*To Marie,
Love and prayers,
Lois Clymer*

Searching for the Sacred

My Life on a Homestead

LOIS CLYMER

husband, Jim Clymer, PA lawyer

WESTBOW
PRESS®
A DIVISION OF THOMAS NELSON
& ZONDERVAN

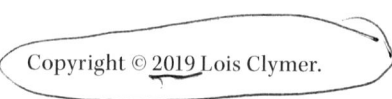
Copyright © 2019 Lois Clymer.

All rights reserved. No part of this book may be used or reproduced by any means, graphic, electronic, or mechanical, including photocopying, recording, taping or by any information storage retrieval system without the written permission of the author except in the case of brief quotations embodied in critical articles and reviews.

WestBow Press books may be ordered through booksellers or by contacting:

WestBow Press
A Division of Thomas Nelson & Zondervan
1663 Liberty Drive
Bloomington, IN 47403
www.westbowpress.com
1 (866) 928-1240

Because of the dynamic nature of the Internet, any web addresses or links contained in this book may have changed since publication and may no longer be valid. The views expressed in this work are solely those of the author and do not necessarily reflect the views of the publisher, and the publisher hereby disclaims any responsibility for them.

Any people depicted in stock imagery provided by Getty Images are models, and such images are being used for illustrative purposes only. Certain stock imagery © Getty Images.

Scripture quotations taken from the New American Standard Bible® (NASB), Copyright © 1960, 1962, 1963, 1968, 1971, 1972, 1973, 1975, 1977, 1995 by The Lockman Foundation Used by permission. www.Lockman.org

ISBN: 978-1-9736-7289-0 (sc)
ISBN: 978-1-9736-7288-3 (hc)
ISBN: 978-1-9736-7290-6 (e)

Library of Congress Control Number: 2019913474

Print information available on the last page.

WestBow Press rev. date: 10/02/2019

Contents

Introduction vii

Chapter 1   The Dream 1
Chapter 2   Our First Little Homestead 7
Chapter 3   A Perfect Piece of Land 17
Chapter 4   Our Many Animal Friends 25
Chapter 5   Growing Food 31
Chapter 6   Flowers and Politics 37
Chapter 7   Cooking and Preserving Food 43
Chapter 8   Nature Trails 51
Chapter 9   Our Mini Homesteads Away from Home 57
Chapter 10 Entertainment on and off the Homestead 63
Chapter 11 Selling Vegetables and Flying in a Private Airplane 71
Chapter 12 Building Tiny Houses 81

Appendix 1 87
Endnotes 101

Introduction

A Dream is a wondrous thing. As newlyweds my husband and I developed a dream. I think it started when we were invited for Sunday dinner to the home of a young couple who attended the church we had begun attending.

After a delicious meal and friendly chit-chat, we were led to their back yard and what we saw there impressed us both. A gorgeous little homestead laid out with a perfect little garden and luscious looking grapes along with a stream meandering through the property. Chickens and dogs and children seemed to be everywhere. There was something idyllic about the scene and we decided that was what we wanted—our own little homestead with lots of animals and children.

It would be quite a few years before we started looking for our own little homestead. Meanwhile we moved to a very suburban house in Colorado and after several years there we settled in a townhouse in Kansas while my husband went to law school.

This book is the story not only of the homesteads my husband and I built through the years but of the challenges we met along the way and the lessons we learned. I have learned some bits of wisdom over the years which I share at the beginning of each chapter and throughout the book.

Along with the character I attempted to build within myself, I searched for answers to some of life's ultimate questions such as "Why are we here?" and "What is our purpose?" I share some of these answers and what these discoveries meant to me.

Chapter 1

The Dream

Hard work can bring satisfaction and contentment.

We are not certain when our dream was completely formed, but sometime early in our marriage we had decided we definitely wanted a homestead. What is a homestead? The dictionary simply defines it as "a house, especially a farmhouse and outbuildings." Another definition for homesteading is "a lifestyle of self-sufficiency, characterized by subsistence agriculture, home preservation of foodstuffs and sometimes small-scale production of sellable items."

The warm homestead of the couple from our church was impressed in our minds. The stately trees, the neat garden rows, the gurgling stream, and the animals roaming freely seemed at one with the young children who ran among them. For us, this homestead captured a certain serenity and nostalgia often lost in the bustle of modern life.

We started to fill in the outline of our dream. We would buy some land, with a creek flowing through it, and we would have chickens and goats, and beautiful vegetable gardens. Trees were a must and also perhaps a woods. And we would have a lot of children to enjoy our homestead with us. We were not especially attracted to the extremes of self-sufficiency but taking care of some of our food needs was appealing.

"We will grow grapes and maybe raise honeybees," Jim mused.

"And we will have a lot of flowers," I added.

We read books and magazines about homesteads and self-sufficiency. I found one about four-seasons gardening and discovered so many ideas that one could live a lifetime on a homestead and always have something new to try.

Actually, we both grew up on farms where we had experienced some of this lifestyle. Life on a farm, especially a small farm, has a certain rhythm to it, a pattern that repeats itself year after year. It reminds me of the liturgical year of some churches which always has something to commemorate or celebrate. On a farm one's life is governed by the calendar of planting, harvesting, and preserving food. It seems that work is always beckoning; today is the time to plant corn, today the raspberries should be picked, or today we can tomatoes. It may look like a lot of work, but it brings a certain freedom with it. One chooses his own schedule and most things can wait a day or two.

I was surprised when reading about the ancient Egyptians that many of them lived a certain subsistence style existence with their own gardens and animals such as sheep and goats. The very early civilizations that archaeologists have discovered in India along the Indus River had some indications of two- and three-story homes with courtyards, wells and places for vegetables and animals. Down through history subsistence living with small farms has been the norm. As recently as 1800, eighty percent of Americans lived or worked on farms. A small farm is also an ideal place for raising children. They can be with both parents much of the time and there is always something interesting happening. The community life of a farm is warm and nurturing and includes relatives, neighbors, salesmen, harvesters and other farm workers.

Searching for the Sacred

Farming may seem like a lot of work, but there is also a certain pleasure and satisfaction that comes with meeting your own needs for food. I recall running down the basement stairs just to look at my rows of canned vegetables, fruits and jams. Hard work never bothered my husband Jim. He can work harder than any other person I know. Cutting and splitting wood seems like a job just made for him.

I like to collect cookbooks and one of my favorite cookbooks is *Recipes and Remembrances from an Eastern Mediterranean Kitchen* by Sonia Uvezian. She explains what they ate and how they grew and preserved their food. She describes the irrigation practices and gardens of her extended family and her vivid word pictures beautifully bring to life a subsistence living, with its own calendar. I could picture her delight as a child running through the gardens and watching the grownups at work, basking in the security of community and the familiar patterns of work and life.

Yes, most of us today have a style of life that revolves around working for employers far from home. But Jim and I wanted to create perhaps just a touch of a lifestyle from the past. Our efforts brought Jim and me much contentment and helped to cement our lives together. Because partners spend so much time away from each other today, they have less time to form those strings that tie them together. Our homestead was a way to strengthen our marriage, to create the hundreds of tiny threads which sew people together through the years.

There is something about a piece of land or a home that provides security and the longer one lives in the same home, the deeper that security grows. There is something about roots that is unexplainable. Talk to an old-timer who has lived at the same place for a lifetime and you can understand the reverence he feels for a piece of land. Home can be a salve for pain, for failure, and for discouragement. I have always felt I could not live somewhere that I had no dirt of my own to stand on.

We had our dream, but we did not have our homestead before our children started coming. Our oldest, Steve, was born in Pennsylvania before we moved to Colorado. He was a very curious little boy, enjoying every minute of life as children do, and I remember how he used to "fall" into the toy box headfirst before he was tall enough to crawl in, and then he would come out the same way. That curiosity would lead him later to read the World Book encyclopedia. As one of their first grandchildren, Steve was adored by my parents, and he also received much attention from Jim's parents. It was difficult to leave those relationships when we moved to Colorado, but adventure beckoned.

2, Rachel, our only daughter, was born in Colorado. She was feisty and active and never had any difficulty keeping up with her brothers. She had a tremendous love for animals and when we finally settled on our homestead, she could always be seen with some cat, kitten, dog, or puppy. I remember a pair of gerbils that she loved dearly even though one bit her finger one morning. She quickly forgave her little pet.

3, Justin, our second son, was born while my husband Jim was in law school in Topeka, Kansas. I remember what a fast learner Justin was, talking in complete sentences before he was two. As he grew older, he was the one who would read all the notes he would find around the house. He always seemed to know what was going on and any plans we had.

4 Our fourth child, Daniel, was also born while Jim was in law school. He was a sweet natured child who was always smiling. Later when he went to school, it seemed like everyone wanted to be his friend, and I could understand why. With older brothers and a sister to look up to, Daniel was always trying to be like them. He would flip through the pages in a book without pictures, pretending he could read.

Hard work is the secret to success. I soon found that it helped to be organized and to prioritize. When I did the most important thing first in the day, the rest of the day flowed more smoothly. If I didn't do the most important thing first, I found it might get squeezed out and never get done. I loved to make lists (and I am still a list maker) and I learned how to make the list work for me and not just frustrate

5- Jonathan p.11

me. When I made a list for the day, I would look over it and pick out the most important item and do that first. If that item was the only thing on the list that I accomplished that day, I learned that it didn't matter because I had done the most important first.

As a girl, I sometimes had the job of picking tomatoes in the hot sun. Even on the days that I became sore, hot, and as itchy as could be, I would break into a sort of rhythm that enabled me to enjoy the job. I can recall Jim saying that he never had a job he didn't like, and he had quite a few jobs as a young man including driving truck, farming, doing carpentry, and delivering furniture. Jim can work from the time he gets up until he goes to bed. I can't. But I did learn to enjoy work.

It strikes me that the more often one does a job, the more one enjoys it. I am surprised by how much I enjoy washing dishes now and I don't think I did when I was young. The bottom line is that I learned to work, and I am glad I did.

As a young couple, Jim and I had adopted the Christian beliefs we had been exposed to in Christian homes. As we got older and went to college and read a lot, we sometimes asked ourselves if what we had been taught was true. It was certainly very easy living in this culture to see that not everyone believed in Christianity. I remember a discussion I had with Jim when we were in our early twenties. I asked Jim what he based his belief on. He said that first it was very easy for him to believe that there is a God, a power higher than ourselves, because of the amazing world we live in. It was easy to believe that God had created the world. Building on that, Jim said it seemed to him that if God created us, he must have had a purpose for doing so, and it seemed natural that God would communicate it to us through the Bible.

Nature has always appeared to me to be full of miracles. In fact, everything about life and nature seems like a miracle to me. I constantly wonder at the instincts of animals and birds. We find some people today who are trying to make science explain everything and in so doing they push God and miracles out of the picture.

Currently there are many things which have been written opposing Christian beliefs. One idea which I came across was the idea that Christianity was copied from pagan myths. I wondered where that idea had come from and eventually, I found an answer. But it took quite a long time and involved finding some fortunate eye-opening books.

Chapter 2

Our First Little Homestead

"Each day is God's gift to you, Make it blossom and grow into a thing of beauty" –taken from a wall plaque in my bedroom.

As the end of law school grew near and my husband was offered a job back in our hometown in Pennsylvania, Jim and I started thinking about finding that perfect little homestead. After we did some inquiring, a five-acre property with an old farmhouse and a big barn caught our attention. It was scheduled to be sold at auction in the near future. It seemed to be just what we were looking for, possibly at a price we could afford, but we were not able to go look at it or be at the auction.

"Should we get my dad to bid on it and buy it sight unseen?" we asked ourselves. It seemed a bit preposterous, but we were risk takers and that is what we did.

We told my dad how much to bid on the property. On the day of the auction two people in Kansas who had never seen the property were anxiously awaiting the results. We got the property! It sold for $58,000, which seems like a low price to us today, but was a king's ransom to us back then. When law school ended, we packed our belongings in a U-Haul and our four children in our car and headed back to Pennsylvania and our new property—our own little homestead.

I can still remember our first look at the property. I didn't like the fact that the house was close to the road, but I loved everything else. Excitedly we ran over the five-acre property with many exclamations of "Look at this." The land was fairly flat, and it had a large garden that looked like it had been growing things for a long time and we knew that meant fertile soil. That garden would become the envy of the neighborhood (according to some neighbors) as Jim planted and cultivated it. I helped with harvesting and preserved many vegetables by freezing. Sometimes relatives would come to help prepare vegetables for freezing, especially corn. The children would run and play while the grownups worked together and chatted. I recall one time when my mom and dad came to help us freeze twenty dozen ears of corn. The corn had to be picked from the stalks, husked, blanched (put in boiling water for several minutes) and then cut off the cob. It was a lot of work, but the corn sure was delicious and we enjoyed it all winter.

Our children were immediately exploring the big barn and climbing on its rafters. Apparently, Justin, our second son, had no fear of heights. The stories the children tell now make their adventures sound very dangerous. One time the children found a six-foot-long black snake in a bird's nest in the barn. Thankfully, black snakes do not have a poisonous bite. Our barn became the home of chickens, cows, and even one pig.

There was a little creek which ran across the bottom of the property with a little foot bridge across it. Beside the creek was a stand of brush about 10 feet tall. "I think that stand of brush is mostly young locust trees," Jim told me one day. "I bet if I thinned it out, we might have a nice little woods someday."

"That sounds great!" I loved the idea of a woods. And that is exactly what happened. Each year we saw our "little woods" get taller and taller until it really did look like a woods. We were so proud of it because we felt like we had started our own forest. The children played a game in the woods which Steve says he learned from the boy scouts. The one who was "it" would sit quietly in the woods while the others would see who could sneak the closest without being seen.

There was a small wash house behind the house which we never used, but the children certainly did. It was their "club house," their "ghost house," or their "hideaway" —whatever their play demanded. And there were good trees for climbing; in fact, each child claimed his or her own tree.

One of the first things Jim did was to plant an orchard. He bought a used Allis Chalmers tractor to mow the orchard and it seemed there was always some child riding along with him on the tractor. Our daughter particularly enjoyed riding along with Jim on the tractor as he mowed the meadow or the orchard. When Jim would trim the orchard, he would make huge piles of brush which he then burned. The children loved watching the pile burn, with huge orange flames shooting high in the air. When we moved from that homestead six years later, it was hard to leave that orchard.

One curious thing I remember about that house was my little sun spot at the back door stoop. For some reason, because of the way the buildings lay, it was protected from the wind, and because it faced south it was warm all winter long when the sun was shining. I have always gravitated to sunny spots, whether inside the house or outside. Of course, this spot also generated plenty of play time with the children, especially with cats and dogs, puppies and kittens. It seemed there was always a child sitting there with a pet in their arms. We had several German Shepherd dogs to which Jim gave German names such as Greta and Gerta. On the front porch a swing hung from the ceiling. The children loved to swing and so did I.

Jim bought some chicks and soon we had a flock of laying chickens which provided us with eggs. At one time we had several geese roaming the property. Geese can protect a property because they can be vicious to strangers. After you've experienced geese chasing you, you certainly will avoid them in the future. I don't recall having the geese very long. We also had a brownish red pony named Ginger for a little while. The children loved to ride the pony, but he did not cooperate very well. I recall Steve and Justin sitting on the back of that pony coaxing it out to the end of the meadow. It took a lot of persistence to get it to go the 250 yards to the end of the meadow, but when they turned the pony to head back to the barn, he would run fast. The boys loved it.

The children all rode tricycles and scooters and "big wheels" when they were young and then graduated to two wheeled bicycles as soon as they were able. Riding a regular bicycle seemed so grown up compared to the three wheeled cycles. I remember one time our oldest son Steve rode his bicycle to my parents' farm which was about eight miles away. My parents had a poultry farm with large chicken houses. My dad also had a grain drying business and he had a grain elevator with a tower that reached about thirty feet into the air. The children liked to climb that tower on a ladder that was attached to it. It was a thrill to be so high in the air.

Our house had a very antiquated kitchen with old cupboards and an old enameled sink, which we eventually remodeled. The new kitchen was installed in the middle room which had previously been used for a dining room. My brother Lester who is a professional cabinet maker, crafted and placed the new cabinets in place. It was probably forty years ago, but recently he told me that he still remembers that when they carried the first cabinet to our porch and then went back to their truck for the next cabinet a strong gust of wind knocked the first cabinet over. Concerned that the cabinet had been damaged, they carefully set it upright, but it had sustained no damage.

There was a basement where the kids used to roller skate and ride tricycles. Even though they went around and around in a small circle, they still loved it. They also had big yellow Tonka trucks which they would put a knee in the truck bed and push around the cellar and also the yard outside.

We had a tradition of eating pancakes on Saturday mornings. I think that tradition may have been sparked from a favorite book, called "Johnny Orchard and the Bear." I read it to the children so many times that we all had it practically memorized. It was a delightful tale of a small bear who was found in the family's orchard and became a family pet. But when it got too big, it became a problem, and Johnny set out into the woods with the intention of killing it. In the end the bear was caught in a huge log "trap" which some zookeepers had set and the whole family would be able to visit him in the zoo. Some memorable lines from the story which we all would quote in different situations include, "Better a bear in the orchard than an Orchard in the bear," "The bear liked the pancakes on Sunday morning," "Johnny said he would do it," and "They didn't have to go very far, but somehow they kept walking."

Another tradition our family enjoyed was making raised doughnuts when the first winter snowfall came. I used a recipe handed down from my grandmother. Waiting for the dough to rise and cutting out the doughnuts with a round doughnut cutter (with a hole in the center) and then deep fat frying them was a delightful way to spend the day with the snow falling outside.

We were living on our first homestead when our fifth child, Jonathan, was born. We affectionately called him "Johnny." Jonathan was sickly from birth. He was small at only 4 lb. 13 oz and he just didn't seem to grow. The doctors didn't know why. We hoped for the best and thought maybe he would outgrow whatever his problem was. Our other four children were healthy. I remember one time taking Jonathan to see a new doctor and taking my 2-year-old and 4-year-old with me so the doctor would see that Jonathan's problem wasn't just that I didn't know how to care for a child. They were the picture of health—bouncy, happy, and talkative little tykes.

One day during this time I picked up the phone and a pleasant voice with a delightful New England accent asked, "Are you Lois Clymer?"

"Yes," I replied. She told me her name and then hurried on with her offer. "My name is Susan. I am part of a Bible Study in the Lancaster area and your name was mentioned as someone who could use a little help. I understand you have four small children and a sick baby."

"That's true," I said.

"I moved here from Boston because of my husband's job and I miss my grandbabies back in Boston and I would like to come and help you one day a week."

I was astounded. I hardly knew what to say. Here was a woman whom I had never met offering to come and help me. "Well, yes," I stammered, "I could use some help."

I gave her my address and a couple days later she stopped by. She was an attractive woman, probably at least twenty years older than me. She had a beautiful smile that lit up her whole face and I loved her accent. She met my children including Jonathan and we arranged for her to come one day a week and watch the children for several hours. She became a life saver for me and I have always thought of her as my "angel."

When she would come, she would shoo me out the door, saying, "Just go and relax. Do whatever you wish and come back in several hours." I remember how strange I felt the first time she came and I got in the car without any children, like something was missing. But I thoroughly enjoyed those days. I would go shopping—sometimes for groceries and sometimes for other things. I would visit a friend or my parents.

She was a capable person, obviously, to be able to care for five children. She had had eight children of her own and had several grandchildren whom she missed dearly. She read books to the older children and played with Jonathan. Since Jonathan never seemed to have an appetite, she would try to coax him to eat.

Sometimes I would come back a little early and we would talk. I found her to be very likable, gentle, and unassuming. She had a strong faith in God. She loved our little "homestead" and she always admired our large garden. One time she helped me pick strawberries.

When Jonathan became sick and was hospitalized, Susan came and helped with the other children. At this time all of the children were sick. I wondered if they might have gotten some kind of food poisoning. My husband and I were in the hospital with Jonathan and we kept checking on the other children who were vomiting and had diarrhea. When we realized that Jonathan was dying, the thought struck me that maybe I was going to lose all my children. But thank God, they got better and were soon over whatever the illness was. The doctors determined that Jonathan had a kidney problem but was too small for a transplant, and dialysis was not an option.

Knowing your eighteen-month-old child is dying and nothing can be done to stop it is a terrifying feeling. Our pastor comforted us by telling us that he would gain more in heaven than he ever could have in this world: "What he will experience in heaven compared to a whole life here is the difference between a drop and a whole bucket of water." Somehow those words comforted me. But how could I care for a child I knew was dying? We had a porch swing and Jonathan liked to sit on my lap and swing. I decided to arrange my schedule so that I would have time to sit on the porch and swing with Jonathan.

But he never came back home. The doctors decided to do one more test and that test involved withholding water for a period of time and his little body simply shut down. For a long time after his death I pictured the little fellow asking for water and being denied because of the test and it drove me crazy. Why had we let him suffer so? It was his suffering that bothered me.

I never sat on that porch swing again. I left his bedroom just as he left it for a long time. When I drove in the car with the children, I would ask Justin and Daniel to climb into the front seat so we wouldn't miss Jonathan in his little car seat. Back then we used front car seats for infants and very small children, but no car seats in the back.

For weeks and months I tormented myself with the picture of his suffering before he died. Then one day I told myself that I didn't need to grieve anymore. I blocked the thoughts and images from my mind whenever they would come.

Susan moved back to Boston to her children and grandchildren shortly after Jonathan's death. I missed her and have often thought of her with fondness. We communicated several times by phone or letter, but our paths did not cross again. That a woman who didn't even know me would come and give such treasured help at a time when I desperately needed it has always amazed me. There is one incident that happened twenty years after Jonathan's death that places her even more surely as an angel in my mind. Our daughter Rachel, who by this time was married with two small children, developed a brain tumor and needed surgery which was scheduled within the week. We had had no contact with Susan for at least ten years and were surprised by a phone call from her on the second day after Rachel's brain surgery. Susan asked me, "Lois, is everything all right? Your name popped into my mind during prayer time." I told her about our situation, and she promised to pray. Rachel's recuperation was difficult, but as I write this today (twenty years after her surgery) she has almost no lingering effects from the tumor and surgery.

Most of us find that life doesn't always go the way we wanted it to. What do we do when pain and disappointments and grief enter our lives? As a young person, I struggled with how to be happy. Sometimes contentment eluded me, and I was not immune to bitterness. But I learned that I could create my own happiness. I came across some wise counsel regarding happiness. If I am unhappy, I am creating it myself. It is not because of my environment, but because of the way I am evaluating my environment. This is why some people can be quite content while others are miserable in somewhat similar circumstances. It comes down to what I expect from life and to what my purpose is. One day I sat down and thought about what I wanted to accomplish during my life. After being encouraged by an inspirational speaker to do so, I wrote a mission statement. All businesses have mission statements and as a wife and mother I certainly was running a rather complicated business. I wrote this mission statement when I was about thirty years old:

> To show love and faith in God to my family.
> To work productively.
> To reach out and help others.
> To create a peaceful, beautiful home and garden.
> I recognize that I can choose my attitude and that circumstances and other people are not responsible for the quality of my life.
> I will strive to be honest, appreciative, and cheerful.
> I will not waste what I have by being upset over what I don't have.

My mission statement contains worthwhile goals, but I can't say I have always followed them. I have, however, from time to time pulled it out of my jewelry box to read. I have always been impressed by my mother in law's attitudes toward life. She had a contentment about her that enabled her to meet any problem life threw at her without becoming upset or bitter. Her children seemed to catch that attitude. A sister-in-law told me one time that her daughter said to her, "Mom, the problem with you is that you don't know how to stay mad at people!" What a legacy!

Chapter 3

A Perfect Piece of Land

"Bless this house, O Lord we pray, keep it safe
by night and day"—Motto in our house.

"There is a piece of land for sale that I think we should look at," Jim told me one day after work. "I pass it on my way to work and the sign says twenty-two acres." Even though Jim was a lawyer, he was still a farmer at heart. To have twenty-two acres to manage sounded great to him. We contacted the owner and met him at the land. From the road, the lane entering the property looked very steep.

"How could we have a lane so steep?" I asked.

"That could be blasted until it was almost level," the owner replied. Wow! The marvels of modern excavation.

We walked to the top of the hill where there was a little clearing. There were no buildings on the property. The land lay along the Little Conestoga Creek and we followed the creek to a nice sized pond which looked neglected. It didn't have much water in it. There was a lot of woodland and some meadows. Jim loved the property. I liked the idea of building a new house. We found money for a down payment and then we wondered how we could ever afford to build the house.

We sold our dear little homestead. It was sad. But better beckoned. We lived in the suburbs of Lancaster for three years while our house was being built. While we lived there, we bought our first computer, a TRS-80 from Radio Shack. The boys still remember their first Atari which had a joystick with a red button. They talk about Frogger and Pitfall and how you could collect treasures or gold bars. I am sure we did not realize it at the time, but a new age had dawned, an electronic one.

I looked at house plans for a long time before choosing one which I thought would fit the lay of the land. It was a modified A frame and was passive solar. And it certainly has been a passive solar structure. It faces mostly south and slightly southeast, and when the sun shines the large windows of the A frame, reaching to the second story, catch the sun and the heat.

While the house was being built, I came almost every day to watch the progress and enjoy the camaraderie of the builders. First the hole was dug for the basement and the basement walls of cement blocks were laid. Then the frame and windows appeared. It was such an interesting experience to watch the house "come alive" after having chosen the house plan.

We installed a large wood stove in the basement along with a furnace. Jim put an air duct from the wood stove blower into the ductwork of the furnace and we found that we could heat the whole house with that wood stove. Between the sun and the wood stove we paid little for heat. At least not money. Jim has spent hours and hours of hard labor cutting and splitting wood for that stove. Some years later we installed a second stove with a window in it on the main floor next to the fireplace. Sitting next to this stove to watch the flames has become my favorite place to be on cold winter evenings.

The pond on the property seemed to beckon to all of us. "Don't walk there on the ice. You might fall in," Rachel warned her brother Justin as the two of them played near the edge of the pond. Jim had brought the children down to the pond in his old pickup truck while he checked on some dead trees for future cutting.

"Help!" cried Justin as the ice cracked all around him. Fortunately, the pond was not deep there and he was able to get out quickly, but he was soaking wet. He hurried to the pickup truck and sat there shivering while Rachel ran to find Jim.

We wondered why the pond would not stay filled up. There were certainly some springs feeding it. To supplement them, we ran a long line of pipe from our artesian well near the house to the pond. But there was a problem. The pond just would not stay filled up. It seemed to leak.

"I think the problem is that it is right beside the creek which is lower than the pond so the pull of the water in the creek exerts pressure on the water in the pond, pulling it through the soil down to the creek," a friend told us. Water has a way of finding its own level.

"Then we will have to find a way to make the banks of the pond tight," said Jim, determined to make that pond work. And so began the saga of trying to stop the pond from leaking. We had concrete poured on the banks. It didn't work. The pond still leaked.

"Okay, we'll get all the water out and put a black heavy liner on the bottom. Surely water will not get through a heavy plastic liner." Jim was determined. He set up pumps to pump all the water from the pond. When most of the water was out, Jim summoned all the help he could find to try to get the rest of the water out. With boots on, Jim, the children, a few friends, and I mucked around the bottom of the pond, filling buckets with water and dumping them into the creek.

"Hey, you! Take that!" Mud seemed to be flying everywhere. I couldn't figure out if we were having fun or working. Oh well, such is life.

The liner wound up floating to the top of the water in spots and transformed into huge black turtles. We poured sand in the pond to keep the liner down. But the pond still leaked.

Even though Jim never achieved the beautiful pond we had dreamed of, we do have many memories associated with that pond—paddle boating in the summer, skating in the winter, and, perhaps the most exciting, watching a pair of Canada geese make a nest every spring on the banks of the pond. The children found a snapping turtle one time and were impressed that the snapping turtle could break a decent sized stick in half. After that we were cautious about getting into the water. The creek beside the pond gendered its own playtime. The creek was only a few feet deep at its deepest point and just right for wading and tubing and water fun. At one point we bought a canoe and two kayaks to use on the creek. We took them down the creek through adjoining properties several times, but the creek was shallow in so many places that we often ended up carrying the kayaks.

"We need to try the Conestoga Creek instead of our Little Conestoga Creek. That is much deeper," suggested one of the children. We looked at a local map and saw that the Conestoga wound around the countryside before reaching the Susquehanna River. One day we picked a spot to enter the Conestoga Creek and arranged for a pickup not too far from our house. We paddled through the countryside enjoying the sights and sound, but not very sure where we were or how far we were from the pickup site. We had failed to realize just how long it would take as the creek has a very meandering path.

"Look, it's getting dark," I fretted. Soon it was very dark on what was a moonless night. We kept paddling. At some places there were houses with lights near the creek that let us see a little, but in most places it was very dark. It was a huge relief when we finally reached our pickup spot. We discovered that the person waiting for us had become so worried that he had actually contacted the police.

One Memorial Day evening we were on our way home after having dinner with Jim's sister Erma. As we came close to our home, we found the road blocked by police. Jim told them we lived right at the bottom of the hill but was told we could not drive down there. The police said there had been a tornado and a lot of trees were knocked down and that we would be unable to drive up our lane. We have a long driveway, about six hundred feet long. We parked our car at the neighbors and walked down the road to our home. As we got close we saw there were huge trees fallen down everywhere. In fact, we could not even walk up our lane as it was blocked by tree limbs. Many of the old trees which had lined our driveway now lay in a tangled mess. We walked along our neighbor's field, shocked that our whole long driveway seemed to be just filled with fallen trees.

We wondered if our house had been damaged. As we came close to the house, we found that it had not been damaged at all. Relieved that it had escaped harm, we entered the house and looked for some candles to light as there was no electricity. The lane was such a maze of tree branches that one could not even walk through it. The electric lines which ran along our lane were down. Because of those electric lines, our local power company sent crews out to clear the lane. They worked all night and by morning our lane was usable again and we had electricity. In the morning as we explored the rest of our property, we found many trees uprooted, including one below our house which left a crater sized hole. Jim and the boys worked hard cutting up those trees for the next year or two.

Tornados are not frequent in our area, but we certainly experienced a memorable one for us. Some other people also experienced some damage. Parts of roofs were blown off and on a neighbor's property a tobacco shed was lifted up and came down on the roof of a car while a woman in the car watched helplessly. Neither she nor her two children in the car with her had any serious injuries. The tornado damage stretched on a path of about a mile and a half.

Homesteads and barns seem to go together. Every farmer would like to have a barn to keep his animals in and to store grain and farm implements. For a while we made do with sheds and lean-tos, but the day finally came when we would build that big, red barn. The barn was built on the side of a hill so that on the lower side doors were placed where the animals could go in and out and on the higher side there was an entrance to drive the tractor through and to store hay bales.

"It looks like we lost a chicken to some wild animal. I think it may have been a fox," Jim announced one morning after chores. We put a big fence around the barn in an attempt to keep our animals in and the foxes out. It seems like raising animals and growing vegetables is a constant fight with nature. There are wild animals such as foxes and raccoons and also hawks which go after chickens, and there are groundhogs and rabbits which like to eat from the vegetable garden.

A dog can be a farmer's best friend when it comes to chasing off wild animals. We had several over the years, mostly German shepherds, although we also had a Newfoundland named Molly. I remember one-time Molly had three puppies, adorable little black puff balls with short legs but with an exuberance so great that sometimes they would roll over and over as they ran down the yard playing with the children. We also had a beautiful Golden Retriever named Lilly, and a smart Border Collie named Max. After a few dogs were hit on the road and others wondered away into adjoining properties, we installed an invisible fence around our house and garden. This fence worked well because the dog still could easily keep groundhogs and rabbits from our garden. The dog received a lot of attention from the children and liked to be with Jim and me as we worked in the garden. He also received attention from the many visitors a farm has—mail carrier, neighbors, delivery men, salesman, relatives, meter men and so forth.

There are lots of trees on our property and we have one which is a landmark. It is an old, old oak tree which actually is two tree trunks joined at the bottom, each with a diameter of about five feet. Its branches form a huge circle. Jim made a hunting platform in that tree and climbing up to that platform and sitting in the midst of that old tree makes one dream of days gone by. How old is the tree? Surely it was there when the Declaration of Independence was signed. Or maybe not. How does one date trees without cutting them down?

We loved our new homestead but sometimes it seemed the work involved was more than we had bargained for. All days are not sunny ones. Life has its ups and downs and it is easy for spouses to say something to hurt each other. Someone has said that a good marriage involves two people who are good forgivers. Hanging on to grudges or bitterness can be death to a marriage. Jim and I learned that through trial and error. Forgiveness is a huge gift to both the forgiven and the forgiver. Edwin Chapin tells us, "Never does the human soul appear so strong as when it forgoes revenge and dares to forgive an injury."

When we say the Lord's prayer, we ask God to forgive us as we forgive others. Does that mean if we don't forgive others, then God should not forgive us? I was impressed by a message on forgiveness given by Dr. D. James Kennedy. "Suppose," he said, "God said to you and to me, 'Yes, I will forgive your sins, but I am not going to have anything to do with you anymore. I never want to lay my eyes on you again.' Is that forgiveness?"

I have certainly not always been perfect, and I have held onto bitterness from time to time. But I have noticed that when I can release that bitterness and let it go completely, something good happens in my body. My creativity and my joy returns. The antidote to the poison of bitterness is forgiveness and gratefulness. Bitterness can not survive in a heart which is grateful. Gratefulness is a marvelous thing to learn. Not only does it tend to generate happiness, but it tends to give one a pleasant personality.

On the creek beside our homestead

Chapter 4

Our Many Animal Friends

"Happiness is what happens when you get too busy to be miserable"—Anonymous.

"Watch that mother hen," Jim called to me. "See how those little chicks stay right close to her and when she scratches in the dirt and makes an excited clucking sound, the little ones come right to where she had scratched and start pecking in the dirt. I wonder what they are finding."

"I guess it's bugs and insects. But they also seem to be eating grass," I observed. From time to time we would have a mother hen who decided to sit on eggs and brood. Jim would place some more eggs under her, usually about 8 to 10, and sometimes that many would hatch, and the mother hen would start making a clucking sound which she would continue for six to eight weeks. At night the chicks would all crawl under her as she sat on the ground and sort of spread her wings. Then at some point after about six to eight weeks, the mother hen would all of a sudden stop clucking and at that point the chicks would all need to fend for themselves. They no longer crawled under her wings but would now fly up to roost with all the other chickens.

One time we had a duck which hatched two or three eggs but then disappeared, and we were left with one little duckling. At the time we had a mother hen with some chicks.

"I am going to see if I could put that little duckling under the mother hen tonight and maybe she will care for it," Jim told me. And she did! The little duckling would wander over our yard with the mother hen and her chicks.

"Look closely at that little duckling and the chicks," I told the children, "and notice how the chicks will all run to where the mother hen is scratching and peck in the dirt, but the duckling is not interested in that at all, but simply seems to be running around catching bugs in the air."

Most of the chickens we had over the years were not hatched by a hen sitting on eggs. Usually we ordered the chicks online from a supplier and they were sent via the post office. I would get a call from our local post office that the chicks had arrived, and I needed to pick them up. When I would go to the post office, I could hear the chicks peeping somewhere behind the counter. I can remember one time when I went to pick up chicks.

"I came to pick up chicks," I told the clerk.

"O no, now we won't be able to listen to them anymore." Apparently, the clerks were enjoying the chicks. I could understand why. The chicks are only a day or two old when they are mailed in a cardboard carton. We usually ordered about two dozen and as soon as I got them home, I would put them in a larger box with newspaper on the bottom, give them some water and chick feed, and put a light over them to keep them warm. The children loved them too. They run around peeping loudly; little puff balls of fur as the feathers haven't formed yet. Occasionally we would hatch some eggs in an incubator and we were all thrilled to watch the chicks hatch. First a hole would appear in an egg and then it would get larger and larger over a number of hours until finally the chick would emerge. We had a large brooder where we would keep them the first couple weeks. Our brooder is a large low pen about four feet square which is thermostatically heat controlled. The chicks need to be kept at a certain temperature, something which the mother hen's body would do automatically.

I loved our chickens and I liked having our own eggs. I once read that eggs from chickens which are "free range" and are free to eat bugs and grass are healthier. Years later I read that eggs from "chickens on range" (where chickens eat some grass) contain in them a vitamin called K2 which Americans are often missing in their diet. Vitamin K2 was lost when dairy and beef no longer were raised on grass.

Most of our time on our second homestead we have had goats. Jim was hoping they would help to keep the grass eaten around the barn and they did. But goats are browsers rather than grazers and they preferred to eat leaves from the low hanging branches of the trees in our barnyard. They also gnawed on the bark and were hard on the trees. From time to time Jim would give them some tree branches from a tree he had cut down and they acted as if he had given them a real treat.

The goats would generally give birth in the early spring and often would have twins. We usually had three or four or more kids born in the spring who would play and frolic all spring and summer and even into the fall. Kids are some of the most playful animals; their antics and frolicking are delightful to watch. They liked to jump on top of things—logs, barrels, each other, anything. Sometimes I assisted the mother goats when they gave birth. A healthy kid would get to its feet immediately—long spindly legs wobbling as instinct tells it to immediately nuzzle the mother to find milk.

We had periods of time when Jim would milk the goats each morning. He would pen the kids away from their mothers overnight so he could get the first milk in the mornings and then allow the kids to be with their mothers the rest of the day. Jim grew up on a dairy farm, so he found it easy to get milk from the goats. It was a struggle for me; I didn't seem to have quite the right touch. The milk tasted good, not much different from cow's milk.

Several times I made some cheese from the milk. I made a type of mozzarella which tasted delicious. I have also made cottage cheese by simply heating a gallon of milk to 185 degrees and adding one fourth cup of vinegar. The curds form quickly and can be strained from the whey. Another easy recipe for cheese makes a cheese similar to Velveeta. The milk is heated to 140 degrees and 1 tablespoon of citric acid is added. Curds form and the whey is drained. Then one teaspoon soda, one teaspoon salt, and some butter and cream are added to the curds. The mixture is heated and stirred until smooth. Cheese is not difficult to make and there are many different recipes.

"I think I will order some wild type turkeys which I saw advertised," Jim told me one day. He set about building an enclosure around an old shed to keep them in. Watching the turkeys grow was fascinating. When they got old enough several flew away but some of them seemed to be attached to our property and hung around, often resting on the deck railing in front of our house. They were beautiful birds with blue-green shimmering feathers and sometimes when they would sit and puff themselves up and spread their tail, they looked just like the pictures we see of the pilgrims and turkeys at the first thanksgiving. But eventually they all left us. Occasionally when I was driving in the car near our home, I would catch a glimpse of one or two whom I thought might have been "our turkeys."

Sometimes instead of goats we had sheep. Baby lambs are certainly adorable, and sheep are better grazers than are goats. But I found that male sheep were more aggressive than male goats, and I do not like to be around animals that I am afraid of. They are called rams for a reason!

We had various other animals. For a while some heifers (young cows) grazed in the meadow near the pond. At one point we bought a donkey because Jim had heard that a donkey would chase away wild animals such as foxes who come around the barn to get chickens.

In the house we have sometimes had a cat and also a birdcage with two parakeets.

I found our homestead to be a peaceful place where I could rejuvenate my body and soul when needed. Sitting at our breakfast table and watching the chickens scratching in the grass or the kid goats running for the sheer joy of running would simply calm me. The writer of Proverbs tells us that "A heart at peace gives life to the body, but envy rots the bones." Negative emotions are hard on the body and I was not immune to them. Stress and fear and worry would sometimes grip me. Jim and I loved our animals and they often added a needed relief to the pressures of life.

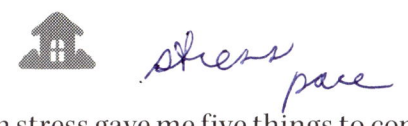

stress pace

A favorite book of mine on stress gave me five things to consider when stress would overwhelm me: 1) Re-label. Ask myself if "the situation was really as bad as I was imagining it to be?"; 2) Change my pace and slow down or speed up as needed; 3) Strengthen my body by exercise and diet; 4) Strengthen my faith in God; 5) Re-organize.

I like to organize, and sometimes simply sitting down and organizing my thoughts and plans helps to combat stress. Another thing I learned was that I needed to set my own pace, one that worked for me. My husband goes eighty miles an hour; he has a very fast pace and always has and probably always will. For a while after we were married, I tried to keep up with him and burnt myself out. I found my own pace eventually and that works very well for us. He goes his pace and I go mine. He no longer expects me to keep up with him but respects my pace. At my slower pace I still get a lot done and feel great satisfaction with my accomplishments.

Feeding baby kids

Chapter 5

Growing Food

*"Enjoy the little things"—Painted on a motto
given me by a granddaughter.*

I made a little furrow in the soil. The little raised planting bed had been carefully cleared of weeds and the soil overturned and then raked. I handed a little bag of seeds to my little granddaughter.

"Place the seeds in the little furrow row about three inches apart like this," I showed her. She carefully placed the seeds in the row. We covered them with some soil.

"Now we will get some water and give them a drink to help them grow." The sprinkling can was fun to use and soon the soil was wet in the little raised bed which I had told my granddaughter could be hers. She had chosen the seeds she wanted to grow. She sat down beside the garden. Later when her parents were ready to leave, she didn't want to go.

"I want to watch my plants grow," she explained.

We told her that they would not grow so fast that she could watch them grow. But she could come every day and see the change in growth as soon as they came up through the soil. There is something fascinating about watching a seedling break through the soil and grow into a strong plant.

Jim has always seemed to enjoy gardening, but it took a while for it to become an enjoyable hobby for me. For many years Jim would plant rows of vegetables such as corn, potatoes, peas, and green beans. When weeding time came, the children helped with that chore. The children also helped to pick the potato beetles off the potatoes and drop then into a little jar filled with some gasoline. My responsibility came when the vegetables were ready to harvest. I would pick the peas or whatever was ready and prepare them for freezing. We would have vegetables in our freezer to eat throughout the year. It was a lot of work but I had learned how to do it from my mother, and I found preserving food to be an enjoyable task.

Later I became more involved in growing things. Each year I would plan carefully in January what I was going to plant. I loved to begin the planning process when the seed catalogs started coming after Christmas. The pictures in the seed catalogs are enticing. I bought a lot of gardening books over the years and when raised bed planting became popular, I tried it and liked it. I now grow some plants in raised beds and some in the kind of traditional rows I was taught as a child.

One of the nice things about gardening is that each year we begin with a clean slate and have a chance to try again. It seems like a lot of us gardeners begin with great enthusiasm in the spring, but by the middle of the summer the garden is neglected and weeds start to take over. I do not like to pull weeds and I have found that mulching my garden carefully in the spring means that I do not need to do much weeding. I usually use hay from the barn stalls to mulch my garden, and it also acts like fertilizer. Leaves make an excellent mulch for gardens and sometimes I collect leaves in the fall to use on my garden in the spring. Another thing that works is grass clippings and since we don't put herbicides on our grass, I sometimes use grass. I have also used newspaper and black plastic.

Searching for the Sacred

I have always tried to stay away from pesticides and chemicals to kill pests in the garden. It is difficult to know whether or not the chemicals we dump onto our growing food will harm our bodies. Ever since I trained as a nurse after high school, I have wondered why people get sick and if there is anything we could do to prevent sickness, especially conditions like heart disease and cancer which are so common in our society. Over the years we have heard many theories about the prevention and cure of these conditions, but often the theories do not pan out and we are left wondering.

A few years ago I came across a book called *Nourishing Traditions* by Sally Fallon. I was fascinated by her idea that our modern diet may have changed in ways that harm us. She took her ideas from Weston Price, a dentist who in the 1930s traveled to all parts of the world looking for people on old traditional diets. He wanted to compare the nutrients in these traditional diets with the nutrients in our modern diet. Weston Price showed that the old diets appeared to prevent tooth decay and the people seemed to be healthier and more immune to disease. He felt that our modern diets were particularly lacking in the fat-soluble vitamins such as Vitamin A and D and one which he couldn't identify which he called Activator X. Activator X was found in butter from cows which eat the fast-growing grass in the spring.

Consuming milk and butter and meat from grass fed animals helps to put that vitamin back in our diets. What Price called Activator X is now thought to be Vitamin K2, a vitamin most people are deficient in. Vitamin K2 is now thought by some to help prevent heart disease and osteoporosis by helping to put calcium in the bones where it belongs instead of in the arteries of the heart.

As explained by Sally Fallon, one of the major changes in our modern diet has been an "oil change." Whereas our great grandparents used animal fats such as lard, beef tallow, and butter for cooking and frying many of us we now use vegetable oil which has been highly refined. This is a big change; as recently as 1990

MacDonald's fried their French fries in beef tallow. We have been told that vegetable oil is much better for us than animal fats. But is it? Vegetable oil tends to make trans fats when it is refined, and it does not contain Vitamin K2. Most of our animal fats do not have much Vitamin K2 anymore either because our animals are now fed grains instead of allowing them to eat grass. I like to make sure that the milk and butter I buy comes from grass fed animals, and I like to fry and sauté with "ghee" (butter which has been purified). I try to stay away from vegetable oils as much as I can, but that is difficult because they are in almost everything.

Finding healthful food is a big issue for me. As mothers we tend to be the guardians of our children's health. It is not easy to tell what is healthful, especially now with all the different theories coming and going. But I felt I should at least try. Following a traditional diet of a long-lived people group seemed to me to be a good bet.

I have learned to enjoy the little things in life, such as observing nature and watching plants grow, blossom, and produce. I learned to enjoy my daily duties and I also tried to do what I felt was morally correct. As I tried to live a Christian life, I wondered sometimes at those who use sarcasm against God and the Bible. Were they so sure that God did not exist that they were comfortable in poking fun at Him and believers? I read some of the things which the skeptics had written. It appeared to me that they had convinced themselves that God did not exist and had set up "straw men" which they could easily tear down. They would interpret the Bible in such a way that they could then say how ridiculous it was. But how could they be so sure they were interpreting the Bible correctly? They seemed to be making themselves "God." Sometimes man's arrogance is terrifying. Each of us is one person out of six billion people living for seventy to eighty years, a mere speck in the fabric of time. There are things which we cannot understand or know. We need to have humility.

Searching for the Sacred

As I pondered ways in which we could know that Christianity is true, I came across some information on the Shroud of Turin, the burial garment of Jesus Christ. The Shroud has been the object of much research in the past century. After studying several books on the subject, I found the shroud to be an amazing witness to the suffering of Christ on the cross and the image on the shroud a witness to his resurrection. The Turin Shroud Center of Colorado has compiled the research done on the Shroud into *The Shroud of Turin, a Critical Summary of Observations, Data, and Hypotheses.* The researchers state that "Dr. Jackson and his TSC associates, after years of intense research following the completion of the STURP project and coupled with the research finding of an ever-expanding body of Shroud scholars, have come to hold the position that the Shroud of Turin is in fact the burial Shroud of Jesus of Nazareth" (97).

The Shroud of Turin helped to solidify my faith and chase away any lingering doubts I had. I thought there must be other things which could tangibly prove Christianity, and I began searching. I specifically wanted an answer to the skeptics who said that Christianity was copied from pagan myths.

The Shroud of Turin

Chapter 6

Flowers and Politics

"Flowers leave some of their Fragrance
in the Hand that Bestows Them."
This is the message embroidered on a
wedding gift from a great aunt.

I have always loved flowers but when I married I did not know much about growing them. I learned by trial and error. One day I came across an article about five perennials which the article said could be the backbone of a flower bed because they came up every year at different times of the spring and summer and had long lasting foliage so they would look good even when not blooming. The five perennials were iris, peony, daylily, phlox, and aster. I immediately planned my flower bed and ordered several plants of each type. I especially loved the peonies which I had for many years. They were large single peonies with white petals and a fluffy yellow center. Beautiful! And they came up every year, like an old friend showing up each year at the same time. One year I planted a pink double peony near them. I was amazed when sometime later I had large single peonies with PINK petals and a fluffy yellow center. Apparently, I had created my own hybrid.

I have a love affair with irises too. They come early in the spring and when I see those big buds, I can't wait for them to appear. My favorites are the white iris and the yellow iris. My yellow iris came from our vacation home in Tennessee near our son Justin's home. Iris are so easy to grow and transplant. I try to thin them out and transplant them every four years.

Daylilies are another of my favorites. I have a collection ranging from almost white to deep golden. I also grow a lavender variety. Because they transplant so easily, I have put them in many different places. You just can't kill a daylily.

"I have a bunch of daylilies that I dug up last week. Would you like them?" I asked a friend at work.

"Sure, I would love to have some daylilies, "my friend responded. For the next several years she sent me photos in the spring of her daylilies.

Even though I had a lot of success with irises, peonies, and daylilies, I was not as successful with my phlox and asters. I discovered I could fill my flower bed with zinnias instead of phlox and have color which lasted well into the fall. Sometime in August I would also buy some asters or mums which would also give bloom and color in the fall, sometimes almost until Christmas. I also like to plant tulips and daffodil bulbs in the fall for early color in the spring. For a long time I had some beautiful yellow tulips which came up beside my white peonies with the yellow centers. The two looked gorgeous together.

I have also enjoyed azaleas, hydrangeas, coneflowers and black-eyed susans. On my wall I have some photos which my daughter Rachel took of black-eyed susans. In one photo Rachel even managed to include a grasshopper sitting on one of the flower's leaves. Now I can enjoy my flowers even during the winter months.

One fall I picked a place for a new flower bed in front of a large propane tank. I tried to hide the propane tank a bit behind a white plastic picket fence. I dug up from my old flower bed six iris plants and six daylily plants. Then I bought six tulip bulbs and six daffodil bulbs to plant among them. I added three ever blooming rose plants next to the white picket fence sections. With twenty-seven plants in a new flower bed I waited for the magic the following spring. I planned to add some annuals then. I was not disappointed. Of course, it usually takes a couple years before a perennial bed reaches its full magnificence, but I greet the appearance of each flower with pleasure.

One year I dug a five-foot circular bed in the mulch in front of our house beside our Chinese dogwood tree and placed stones around the edge. I asked Jim to trim the tree so some light could get through. I picked out three fragrant tea roses, a red one, a white one, and a gold one for the bed. Roses can be difficult to grow, and I have had an uphill battle with those three rose bushes. But still I have had many beautiful roses to admire.

While I am enjoying my flowers and flowerbeds, my husband's hobby is politics. He reads a lot of magazines, listens to lots of news, and seems to always know who our politicians are and what the current issues are. Jim was attracted to the Constitution Party, and spent much time advancing it. We went to a lot of political conventions and meetings. Some meetings were made up of simple folk and others were filled with well-heeled politicians such as you find in the Washington set. I remember some of the meetings we went to were held in expensive hotels and the dinners they served were exquisite. I probably enjoyed the meals more than some of the speeches for I was not as interested in politics as Jim was. I remember amusing myself by thinking about the clothes the women wore. If I found a dress or suit to be particularly attractive, I would draw a picture of it and later when I was home I would try to copy it.

Politics can deal with issues ranging from the economy to morality and everything in between. It seems to me that our religious liberties are threatened today. Sometimes people will say that one can't legislate morality, but the truth is that all the laws we have anywhere represent someone's philosophy or idea of morality. As some philosophers have pointed out, law is always religious in origin and there can be little tolerance within a legal system for competing ideas. Tolerance is often used as a means of introducing a new legal law system. But when new laws are established, the new system will no longer be tolerant of the old system.

Jim was a candidate for office several times as a third-party candidate; and as he campaigned his speeches got better and better. There is nothing like practice for improving any skill, and politicians running for office get a lot of practice giving speeches.

The race which Jim came the closest to winning was a race for county commissioner. We started the campaign by attending a "Get out the Vote" grass roots training weekend at Leadership Institute in Virginia. Jim and I came away with many ideas for strategy. I took an active role in the planning and strategy. The first thing we did was to choose a team with detailed job descriptions. We had a communications director, an artist, a campaign coordinator, a treasurer, a photographer, and a chairman. Our son Justin managed our website.

Some of our team knew and developed a friendship with two newspaper reporters. Reporters are always looking for something to write about and even if they disagree with the issues, they will treat you fairly and give you coverage. We got a lot of newspaper coverage and I am still not sure why. Our issues included lower taxes, eliminating tax funding for a convention center, preserving family farms, protecting private property rights, and promoting pro-life legislation.

Jim participated in various candidate forums and we sent out many press releases. We were in a lot of parades during this race. One time we rode in a friend's convertible along with a grandchild or two. Some of our campaigners would walk along side of the car handing out our literature. Another time we rode in the back of a pickup truck. I remember one parade where we simply walked but wound up with an interesting "companion."

"Oh, look at that goat!" my husband exclaimed as one of our friends joined us leading a goat which carried a sign which read, "Taxes got your goat? Give Clymer your vote!"

We had various campaign slogans and literature. One was a postcard which showed Jim reading a book to two of his young grandchildren with the slogan, "Preserving a rich heritage for our children, not a debt." Another of our slogans was, "Are you tired of special interests running county government and driving up our debt?"

Election day was intense. We thought we might have a chance at winning since everyone needed to vote for two commissioners. But as the results came in and the evening wore on, we realized we would not win, although we did come close. After election night it was back to life as usual.

Chapter 7

Cooking and Preserving Food

Observe the ant which "prepares her food in the summer and gathers her provision in the harvest." Proverbs 6:8

Much of my life has been spent in cooking. Most of my efforts were centered on the evening meal which we called "supper" although it was the biggest meal of the day and probably should have been called "dinner." I learned to cook from my mother, and it was basically a Pennsylvania Dutch meat, potatoes, and vegetable type of cooking. I never gave a thought to what was healthful; I just cooked the way my ancestors had cooked. I did not really connect health with cooking. When we had been married several years, I was introduced to a couple who ran a health food store. In discussions with them I was told that white flour and white sugar were bad for us and were hurting our health. I remember telling my mother what I had been told.

"That is nonsense," she replied. "My Aunt Maud ate tons of sugar and lived to the old age of 95." But I did try to cut back a little on sugar. In my home we had eaten canned fruit with nearly every meal, and when we canned the fruit we added lots of sugar. We also had desserts with nearly every meal. I stopped eating canned fruit and cut back on desserts.

Later I came across the idea that fat was bad for us. The "Seven Countries Study" by Ancil Keys in the 1950s had shown that the countries which ate more fat, especially animal fat, had less longevity. Again, I told my mother what I was reading about fat being bad for us.

"That is nonsense," she replied. "My ancestors fried everything in lard and ate lots of other animal fat and it never hurt them a bit." But I was influenced by this new trend, and I tried to cut back on animal fat. Using less sugar and less fat, I could no longer make my cooking taste as good as my mother's had. The children now loved to go to Grandma's for supper.

Over the years as I have looked at what may be wrong with the American diet, I have concluded that fat is a problem, but not animal fat, or at least not animal fat from animals whose habitat was the traditional farm. Traditionally, cows and beef grazed on grass; and chickens were likely to spend some time on grass also. Somewhere in the 40s and 50s vegetable oil was highly promoted as healthful, and it replaced the time-honored traditional fats of butter and lard. We are only discovering now how harmful the large amount of vegetable oil in our diet may be. For starters, it lacks a certain vitamin, K2, which is needed for heart and bone health. According to some researchers, Vitamin K2 helps to keep the calcium we eat out of our arteries and into our bones, thus preventing heart disease and osteoporosis. Vegetable oil also may upset a balance between so called omega 3 fats and omega 6 fats. This upset balance can help throw our bodies into an inflammatory state, meaning our bodies are quick to create inflammation. Traditional food patterns developed over centuries likely provide the most healthful diet.

We wonder what we can do about the vegetable oils in our food, which are found in nearly all processed food. People are eating out more and more, but this may be a good time to revive the art of home cooking. Then the cook can choose the ingredients. Cooking does not need to be complicated and time consuming. For a long time, I have used a weekly menu plan consisting of one day for chicken, one day for beef, one day for pork, one day for fish, and one day for egg or cheese. I have several different ways to prepare each of these main courses, but often I use simple sautéing. Then I include some vegetables. My schedule works because I am not adamant about keeping it. I just use it as a guide and feel free to change it however I feel at the moment. But having cooked meals for a long, long time I know how freeing it is to know first thing in the morning what I plan to make for supper and have the ingredients available.

Recently I have discovered a plan for breakfast which requires minimal time. In the morning I take about three ounces of a mixture of spinach and kale and sauté it in some good "grass raised" butter or ghee, butter which has been heated to remove all proteins and other ingredients. It has a high smoke point so is excellent to use for sautéing or frying. It lends a delicious flavor to foods. Anyway, back to my greens which I sauté for a couple minutes. I add a little chopped garlic, some dried red pepper flakes and some salt. It is delicious. The kale gets kind of crunchy when sautéed or fried. I like to eat it with soft boiled eggs. You might think that spinach and kale do not sound very good, but you would be surprised how much flavor cooked greens can have, especially when fried in good butter or ghee with spices and garlic added.

In the summer and fall, I freeze and can the extra produce from the garden; and we eat these vegetables all winter long. I usually start with peas in June. I pick them, shell them, and blanch them in hot water, then cool them immediately, place them in plastic bags, and put them in the freezer. I do the same with green beans, lima beans, and then corn. Corn is such a big production that I recall several times my mom and dad came to help. Jim would pull the corn ears from the stalks in the garden. Then we would all husk the corn. When that was completed, someone put the corn through a hot water bath and immediately cooled it. The corn kernels were then cut from the cobs and placed in plastic bags and frozen. It is a lot of work, but that corn is delicious, and the taste has no comparison with what can be bought in the grocery store.

I usually can quite a few quarts of tomato juice. I like my own tomato juice, which I use mostly for cooking, better than any tomato juice I can buy. Making tomato juice is a fairly simple procedure which I learned from my mother. I learned everything about cooking and preserving food from my mother, but my generation has not passed it on to their children. Nowadays, people are more likely to learn to cook from watching a cooking show on TV.

For my tomato juice, I pick the tomatoes, wash them and cut them into quarters and place them in a large kettle along with some carrots, celery, and onion to help flavor them. When everything is soft, I put it through a sieve and then can the juice, adding some salt to each jar.

I have found that one of the easiest ways to preserve tomatoes is to dry them. I have a small electric dryer with six shelves, and I fill them with tomatoes sliced very thin. They dry beautifully in several hours. Occasionally I have preserved green beans and red beets by canning them (putting them in jars and sealing the jars). I also make jam. The very best jam comes from our sour cherry tree, but rhubarb and strawberries are also very good.

Some things I just freeze without doing anything except washing them. I do peppers like this and strawberries and mulberries. We planted two mulberry trees when we first started this second homestead and now, we have mulberry trees growing all over the place. The birds like mulberries and apparently, they carry the seeds. To collect the mulberries, I place a large sheet or tarp on the ground and shake the tree and the mulberries fall onto the sheet.

Preserving food for use in the winter has always seemed like a good idea to Jim and me. Although we are not hard-core subsistence type adventurers attempting to completely live off the land, the idea of being self-sufficient is attractive to us. One time I came across a book by Carol Deppe called *The Resilient Gardener: Food Production and Self-Reliance in Uncertain Times.* The tagline on the cover caught my eye. It read "Including the Five Crops You Need to Survive and Thrive—Potatoes, Corn, Beans, Squash, and Eggs." Carol Deppe is a successful plant breeder who has specialized in developing crops for organic growing conditions for human survival. She explains in her book that in order to survive in difficult times one needs to grow crops which can provide calories, not just salads. She says people should know how to do this. I thought about the crops which we grew, and my parents grew, and realized that these four crops along with chickens and eggs are what we have been growing. Stored potatoes and squash provide food through early winter and can even last past Christmas. We store potatoes in the cold part of our basement, and I store butternut squash on some bookshelves in our office and they keep most of the winter. Carol Deppe suggested that when the potatoes and squash are used up, a self-sufficient grower could depend on dried beans and dried corn, which can easily be ground into flour. I have never dried beans or corn, but I have frozen large amounts of beans and corn.

Deppe tells us that there is no crop as easy to grow on a small scale as potatoes or that yields as many calories along with a fair amount of protein. Potatoes can survive many kinds of horrid weather that can destroy grain crops. In addition, potatoes are delicious. It is a good idea to know how to be self-sufficient even though hopefully it will never be needed.

The garden occupies a lot of our time in the spring, summer, and fall. What do I do in the winter? Winter is a time for sewing and knitting and reading. I like to sit by a cozy fire and read. I am an avid reader and I have read many books. When I was younger, I liked romance books but then as I got older, I gravitated to all kinds of self-help books and to books on philosophy and religion. Looking for solid answers to faith questions, I have read a number of books on Christian apologetics (why Christianity is true). I thought there must be other things besides the Shroud of Turin which we could experience to strengthen faith. I had read a book by Dr. D. James *constellations*

Lois Clymer

Kennedy called *The Real Meaning of the Zodiac* which shows that the stars in the sky present a Christian message. I wondered if it could really be true, so I reread the book. In the back of the book eight books were listed from which Dr. Kennedy had drawn his information. I ordered several of them to research the topic further.

One of the books was *Mazzaroth* by Frances Rolleston, written in 1863 and reproduced by Kessinger Publishing. As I studied her book, I came to the conclusion that there were several constellations which had an undeniable connection to the verse in Genesis 3:15 which explains that after the "fall of man" God tells the serpent (Satan): "And I will put enmity Between you and the woman, And between your seed and her seed; He [Christ] shall bruise you on the head, And you shall bruise him on the heel." Christians call this verse the Protoevangelium or "first gospel." As James Ryrie states in his Ryrie Study Bible: "Christ, will deal a death blow to Satan's head at the cross, while Satan would bruise Christ's heel (cause him to suffer)."

This explicit symbolism, that of the seed of the woman (the coming Redeemer) bruising the head of the serpent (Satan) while being bruised in the heel, can be found several times in the constellations. In the constellations Satan can be represented by a serpent, a scorpion, or a dragon. One example is Ophiuchus, the Serpent Holder, who is struggling with a huge serpent. His one foot is near the head of the scorpion while his other foot is near the stinger tail of the scorpion. Another example is Hercules. Hercules has one foot on the head of Draco, the Dragon, while in his kneeling position his other foot is held up, as if hurt. The constellations Orion and Perseus also show the theme of "conqueror of the serpent." In her book, Rolleston shows how the names of the stars further explain this interpretation. The constellations are very old and the same or similar constellations are found in all parts of the world showing they had a common origin in very ancient times. When the Greek and Roman myths were later attached to the constellations, they helped show the meanings the ancient men had attached to the figures. A number of famous astronomers have remarked on the great antiquity of the constellations.

In Rolleston's book I came across a statement which made me stop and ponder: "Like others of the skeptic school, Volney reports everywhere in antiquity the existence of the tradition of the expected conqueror of the serpent, a divine person, born of a woman, who was to come; and sees this tradition reflected in the constellations, but why it should be there he does not say" (Part I, p. 19). I found that other historians, both Christian and non-Christian, found the pagan myths to be copied from the constellations.

I recalled that the skeptics, including Volney, had written that Christianity had copied from the pagan myths. Now I was seeing that those pagan myths were copied from the constellations. The important question now became, "How did the constellations get this message?" Rolleston tells us that according to Jewish, Persian and Arabian writers, the family of Seth (Adam, Seth, and Enoch) invented astronomy. There is a reference in *The Antiquities of the Jews* in which the first century historian Josephus credits Seth and his children with the invention of astronomy (*The Complete Works* translated by William Whiston. Nashville: Thomas Nelson, 1998. P 36).

It made sense to me to draw the sequence this way: Early men, aware of the message of a redeemer put the symbols in the sky via the constellations showing the "conqueror of the serpent theme" and the pagan myths copied the theme of a coming redeemer.

In contrast, the sequence the skeptics presented made no sense to me: Christianity copied from pagan myths that had been copied from constellations whose ideas were simply fabricated.

Christians through the ages have recognized that the story of Jesus begins not in Bethlehem but at the beginning of man's time on earth. I wrote a book on these ideas called *Sacred Strands: The Story of a Redeemer Woven Through History*. In the appendix of this book, I include the introduction and first chapter of that book.

Chapter 8

Nature Trails

*"I think that I shall never see a poem as lovely as a tree. . .
Poems are made by fools like me, but only
God can make a tree." Joyce Kilmer*

Trees! How we love them. We have many trees on our property. We have a path through the trees that meanders along our creek for about a half mile. We can begin the path right below the barn yard, but it is treacherous until we get to our pond and then it widens into a path that a tractor could mow.

"Make sure each foothold is secure and hold onto the tree branch here or you will slide into the creek," I warned my young son as we picked our way along the path. It was especially difficult when the soil was wet from rain or snow. We would give a sigh of relief as we reached the pond and no longer were in danger of falling into the creek. I was certain that sometime someone would fall into the creek, but I don't recall that anyone ever did. We had a German Shepherd dog who could traverse that path with ease, and she loved it. At one spot along the trail was a place where the creek had made a little island; small shells were buried all over that island. It was fun wading in the water around that little island and collecting little shells.

"Let's go out to 'cove island' and collect shells," my grandsons would say. We have had many excursions walking along the creek, looking for shells hidden in the dirt. "Treasures" (ranging from dirty bottles and bits of broken glass to old sunglasses) are washed down the creek during high rainy seasons when the creek rises and becomes a roaring, fast moving stream. I warn the children not to go in the water at those times.

"Do you want to go on a walk," we asked a group of visiting friends. We skipped the difficult trail along the creek and instead used the tractor path behind the barn.

"Look, there are some raspberries here." We picked some of the tasty berries. I decided to come back later with a bucket and pick some more. I think black raspberries are my favorite fruit. Black snakes must like berries too because one time I saw a black snake in a tree which had some blackberry bushes reaching into the tree branches. Berries grow wild and it seems like one can never be sure where they will be growing from year to year. Some years they seem to grow better than other years.

"Let's take a tent out to the back trail and sleep overnight in the woods," suggested one of my sons. Two of the boys did. Finding a flat spot to place a tent is always difficult on our rocky land but sleeping in a tent puts one close to nature. The sounds of the night include the crickets and the night owls. The creek murmurs as water flows over rocks. Fireflies buzz around giving off their little sparks of light.

We have a number of tree stands for hunters in our woods. The high stands seem to beckon to our grandchildren to climb them. One stand is in the huge oak tree at the border of our property. Deer can be a real menace in our garden each summer. Jim usually kills a deer each fall for our meat, and we butcher the deer ourselves. First Jim guts the deer and then he hangs it in a tree to skin it. Sometimes if it is cold enough, we leave it hang for a few days to age the meat.

Searching for the Sacred

Then we cut the deer into sections and cut the meat off either in the garage or the basement. We make a lot of it into hamburger by putting it through a heavy-duty meat grinder which we bought several years ago. Before we bought the grinder, I used to take some of the meat to a local butcher to have it ground up. When the meat is ground up, I package it, putting one-pound amounts into each plastic bag. I also package the tenderloin and a few steaks. The venison does not taste much different from beef. Our local deer probably eat a lot of corn and soybeans which are abundant in this farming community, and I think that may make their meat taste less gamy.

One thing which I want to do is to collect as many leaves as possible along with the bark from the tree the leaves come from, identify them, and put them into a notebook. Leaves are amazing. In the spring it is fascinating to measure the growth of the leaves and in the fall to watch the different colors make the whole landscape beautiful. Being able to identify wildflowers and wild edible plants would be nice. I would also like to be able to identify more birds. The possibilities for enjoying nature are endless. I want to build a bird feeder to attract birds closer to our house. I also may build or buy some birdhouses. Some birds can be useful for eating pests that attack our garden plants. Watching animals such as squirrels, rabbits, and deer adds to the enjoyment of nature. We had a beaver for a while, but we could not see him; we could only see the results of his work. Foxes and raccoons have from time to time stolen a few of our chickens.

Another part of nature which I have learned to enjoy is the stars. Stargazing is a wonderful pastime. As I learn to recognize the constellations and see them move throughout the seasons, I find that at each season the familiar ones in the evening sky are like old friends coming back to visit. In order to recognize the constellations, I learned a few common ones such as the Big Dipper, Cassiopeia, and Orion and from them I can find other constellations. I also learned a few landmarks such as the winter triangle, the summer triangle, and the Great Square.

Everyone could learn to recognize a dozen or more constellations. It is not hard. Here are the basics I learned for each season. (You can download a free star chart, Uncle Al's Star Wheel, www.aosny.org/Starwheel.pdf which will help you to locate and recognize the constellations.) The evening winter sky has more bright stars than any other. You can locate Orion easily by the three bright stars which form his belt. There are two stars which mark his shoulders and two more which mark his legs. From his belt hangs a sword which contains the Great Orion Nubula, a cluster of stars which appears as a fuzzy spot. Orion's right shoulder is a bright red first magnitude star called Betelguese. Betelguese is a supergiant star which is 400 times the sun's diameter. After you locate Orion, you can find the winter triangle which consists of Betelguese in Orion, Procyon in the Little Dog, and Sirius in the Big Dog. When you have found this triangle, you can then identify the Little Dog and the Big Dog. You may be able to locate the constellation Gemini (the twins), by finding two bright stars above Orion which are the heads of the twins.

The spring evening sky does not have as many bright stars as the winter evening sky, but there are two which can be found by first locating the Big Dipper. Continue the ARC of the handle of the Big Dipper to find ARCturus, a bright star in Bootes and from there SPIKE down to Spica, the bright star in Virgo.

The summer evening sky has three bright stars which are called the Summer Triangle. Once you locate this triangle, you can find Cygnus (the swan), Aquila (the eagle), and Lyra (the lyre). Cygnus contains the bright star Deneb, which is the high corner of the triangle (that is, the first to rise on the horizon for a North Hemisphere viewer). Vega, the bright star of Lyra, and Altair, the bright star of Aquila, then complete the triangle.

In the autumn evening sky, the Great Square of Pegasus is the landmark to look for. The topmost corner of the Great Square is not actually part of Pegasus, but belongs to Andromeda which looks a little like a narrow V. Cassiopeia is easy to locate because it is high

Searching for the Sacred

in the sky and looks like a W. Near Cassiopeia and Andromeda is Perseus, which looks like a crooked Y.

There you have it. Without any difficulty you can learn to recognize these fourteen constellations—Orion, Little Dog, Big Dog, Gemini, Big Dipper, Bootes, Virgo, Cygnus, Aquilla, Lyra, Pegasus, Andromeda, Cassiopeia, and Perseus. You can also learn the names of the eight bright stars I have pointed out. Then you will know more than most people know about the stars and constellations.

One Christmas evening several members of our family headed outside to look at the stars.

"There is Orion. He is easy to find," someone pointed out.

"Yes," I agreed. "Now let's find the Little Dog and below him the Big Dog."

"The stars sure are bright tonight and the sky is clear. But those trees are hiding the horizon," mused my husband.

"I think you should cut those trees down. They are just on the border of the property and then we could plant some slow growing evergreens," I seriously suggested. It has not happened yet, but we still talk about it.

When we vacation in Alaska, we look at the stars. There seem to be more stars because there is not as much light pollution in Alaska. One time we saw a beautiful aurora and in between the streaks of green and pink was Orion. I love looking at the aurora, the Northern Lights. It is incredible to me that God would have made the world and universe in such a way that we get such magnificent displays of color. Sometimes the aurora looks like clouds of color folded into the sky, moving and pulsating.

My son Daniel tried to explain to me what makes the aurora. Electrons, trapped by the Earth's magnetic field, collide with air molecules and excite them. When they return to their previous state, the extra energy is released as colorful photons. The different elements in the air cause different colors. Oxygen causes green and sometimes red, while nitrogen produces blue. Seems like green is the most common of the colors I have seen, but I have also seen pink and white and purple. Perhaps purple comes from mixing red and blue.

We have a vacation home in Fairbanks, Alaska, because my husband loves Alaska. I think it is that "last frontier" sort of thing. It is such a long way to travel from where we live in Pennsylvania, but I sure do love the Northern Lights. That makes the long trip worth it for me. There is a ski lodge not far from our vacation house where we go some evenings when good aurora activity is forecasted. It is high on a ridge with a clear view of the horizon in all directions. We have seen some beautiful displays there.

Our granddaughter in the barnyard

Chapter 9

Our Mini Homesteads Away from Home

*"Keep your face to the sunshine and
you cannot see the shadows.
It's what the sunflowers do." Helen Keller (who was blind)*

We have several vacation homes and wherever we are, our love of the land and nature surface. We own a share in a hunting cabin about a two-and-a-half-hour drive north near Montoursville, Pennsylvania. The eight partners and some of their families use it to go hunting in the fall. Other times of the year we are all free to use it if no one else is scheduled. We sometimes rent it to friends. Usually we have a day in the spring when everyone goes up to clean and cut firewood. My children still have many good memories from their time in that cabin. We would hike during the day and play games in the evening. One time we went kayaking on a nearby stream and another time we went tubing.

"Are you ready to climb the mountain?" was always the question of the morning. There is a very steep (that is an understatement) path up to the ridge. Full of rocks, it is a difficult climb. I considered myself in good shape if I were able to make that climb. And for many years I did, but I would give a big sigh of relief when we reached the top. It seemed like Jim and the boys did not need to stop during the climb up as I did. At the top of the ridge was a trail, much of which was level. We usually went to the right which led to Smith's Knob; to the left led to an area called Rock Ridge. Close to Smith's Knob there was a steep path up to the little summit, and that climb was even harder than the climb up to the ridge, but at least it was much shorter. On top of Smith's Knob was a great lookout over the valley below. The cliff fell sharply, and I always worried someone would get too close and fall. The boys camped on top of Smith's Knob several times. We had some picnics up there, taking up hot dogs and buns and then making a fire to cook them.

Another memory of our Pine Lane Cabin includes the two rope swings on the property: one behind the house, which swung way out over a little cliff, and another one which swung out over the Loyalsock Creek. At the creek the children would swing out and drop into the water. At night we sometimes saw bear and deer through the big picture window in the main room of the cabin. One day we found a rattlesnake near the cabin, and Jim killed it while the rest of us held our breaths.

We also have a vacation home in Tennessee near our son Justin's home, so we are able to spend time with our four Tennessee grandchildren. The house is a simple little house with three bedrooms and a bonus room over the garage. I have always said that the house may be simple, but it has everything. I like the layout with a kitchen and dining room and large living room on the first floor and three nice sized bedrooms upstairs. It has a small deck and a patio with table and chairs. A swing set with a slide attached sits in the yard. We furnished the house so we are able to rent it out as a VRBO (vacation rental by owner) when we are not using it. The bonus room is large enough for a ping pong table and a futon and a daybed. I had fun turning the large closet in the bonus room into a castle for the children to play, complete with a drop-down bridge over the imaginary moat.

Jim was attracted to the large back yard and cut down tree branches and tilled some areas for a garden. He planted two fig trees, two persimmon trees, several fruit trees, and some blueberry bushes. The fig trees have produced delicious figs that everyone hunts for when they are in season. The fig trees usually winter over fairly well in Tennessee which runs about ten degrees warmer than our property in Pennsylvania. We have had some winters though where frost hit the fig trees hard.

We have enjoyed many times with our grandchildren in Tennessee. We went hiking and biking and one time visited an amusement park. One time we went to a Jeep Jamboree and our son Justin drove his jeep through treacherous trails and up steep hills. That is not my favorite pastime, but Justin seems to love the thrill of jeeping.

The town Franklin where they live has many interesting festivals and we have wandered through some of them, enjoying the sights and sounds and of course, always getting good things to eat.

The grandchildren have helped us rake leaves in the fall and carry branches to the curb when Jim trims the trees. There are a lot of old trees in the backyard. Jim needed to thin out the branches on those trees so sunlight could get through to allow the grass to grow better.

Franklin is a lovely place to live with beautiful weather and many interesting stores. It also has a lot of nice restaurants and we have visited many of them with Justin and his family. I remember one restaurant where the young children were given balloons twisted into interesting animal shapes. Laura loved her balloon monkey. Another time we enjoyed watching our tortillas being shaped and the chef even allowed Henry and Laura to shape their own.

Our most recent vacation home is in Alaska. Jim has always loved Alaska, but I told him that I didn't think I could live in Alaska permanently.

"I could probably live there for a few weeks or a month," I told Jim. He thought that sounded great. The next thing I knew we were talking about buying a house there. We went to Fairbanks, Alaska to look for a house twice. I thought maybe we could build a house there, but Jim thought that would be too complicated to build a house with us living so far away.

The house we ended up buying in Fairbanks is a simple split-level house with one bedroom on the upper level and two bedrooms on the lower level. It has a heated garage which is nice for a cold climate like Alaska. The house is on a ridge about five hundred feet higher than the town below it. That means it is warmer than the town since there is often a temperature inversion on cold days. Since the town is surrounded by a ridge, there is little or no wind. The coldest air then settles in the low spots and it becomes warmer on the ridge where the warm air is rising. In the winter when we leave our house and go down to the town below, it is often ten or fifteen degrees colder there.

"How can you stand it up there in the winter? Isn't it cold and dark?" people sometimes ask me.

"Much of the time it doesn't seem worse than winters can be in Pennsylvania," I answer. Even though the sun may not show its face until about 9-10 am and then set at 2-3 pm, there are a couple hours of twilight before the sun comes up and after it sets. In the high latitudes the sun rises and sets at an angle and therefore stays close to the horizon for a longer period. And when the sun is up, it is low on the horizon and shines right in the large windows we have on the house facing south. In contrast, when you are close to the equator the sun "pops" up over the horizon.

"Look at that rhubarb growing along the side of the house," Jim points out to me. I love rhubarb. I hadn't seen anything growing on the property we bought except grass and trees. I wonder what Jim may eventually be able to grow up there. I am sure he will try something. It is curious to me that one time when we were on a cruise which stopped at the Faroe Islands in the Atlantic Ocean between England and Iceland, I saw a lot of homes had rhubarb growing near the house. Apparently, rhubarb is something which grows in cold climates. I looked on the globe and noted that the Faroe Islands and parts of Alaska are on the same latitude.

We have seen nice displays of the aurora (Northern Lights) several times while in Alaska. One time we had about 15 members of our family at our house in Alaska for Thanksgiving. Our son Daniel who works as an aerospace engineer had turned the question of when the aurora would be active into a science. He had calculated months in advance that the activity might be good during Thanksgiving time and that is one reason we were all there. We were not disappointed although there was only one evening the activity was good. I looked out a window and saw a streak around 9 pm. We woke up and bundled up the young children with us and headed up to our good viewing area at the ski lodge ridge.

"Look over there!" were the exclamations heard as we stood on that cold ridge and watched the sky. From time to time we would see a green steak here or there. All of a sudden, the whole sky seemed to be lit up. Streaks of green and pink and yellow and white moved across the sky, sometimes pulsating and moving, and sometimes looking like curtains folded into the sky. Such magnificence!

We see our love of the land among our children, as they create their own paths through life. Our oldest son Steve has a beautiful property right along the Paissaic River in New Jersey. He loves wildlife and loves to kayak on the river and occasionally we join him in kayaking. He built a nice tree house for his boys.

Two of our boys have made some forays into raising chickens. Daniel has a lovely house in Colorado with a beautiful back yard and roaming on that back yard are three chickens which so far have escaped prowlers. They lay lovely green/blue eggs and are loved by my son's two little girls. Sometimes those chickens even enjoy being held.

"Daddy, can I take Rainbow (the hen) into the house so she can see our house and my bedroom?"

"Hmm," replied Daniel, "Well, I guess so, but hurry!"

She was gone for a bit and then breezed back out of the house, still holding Rainbow. Fortunately, there were no droppings in the house.

Justin built a nice chicken coop and had three chickens who were loved by his whole family. Sadly, one day something broke into his coop and killed his chickens. Now the family is considering getting some alpacas to keep wild animals away. I am looking forward to seeing those alpacas running with a miniature poodle named Pumpkin, a large Weimar doodle named Roosevelt, and Justin's kids.

Justin and his jeep

Chapter 10

Entertainment on and off the Homestead

"In This House Of peace and rest, We welcome you Our lovely Guest." Motto in our foyer.

The possibilities for entertainment on our homestead seem endless. There is hiking and canoeing when the weather is nice. There is sledding when it snows and ice skating when it is cold enough. Our boys liked to play baseball and they found places to mark with their plastic home plate and bases. Swinging on a homemade rope swing provides endless daydreaming time for the young and young at heart. Inside we have a ping pong table and lots of table games.

Friends are important and to have friends one needs to be a friend. I have always liked a quote by Norman Vincent Peale on friendship: "Getting people to like you is only the other side of liking them." It is a simple truth that people are attracted to those who admire them and are repelled by those who look down on them.

On our driveway, in the large turnaround space, I painted a large Chartres-style maze. When friends come to our house they usually question us about the maze. "What is that for?" they ask. Labyrinths or mazes have traditionally been used for prayer and meditation, but I have used mine more for exercise. The grandchildren like to play on it, sometimes turning it into an obstacle course with all kinds of objects to jump over. Sometimes they put signs and objects along the way, telling the walker what he needs to do, such as hop, stretch, or make themselves into a tree.

After reading an article about a maze that was being used for exercise, I found a description of how to make one on the internet with a "seed" pattern. I started by placing four sticks in the ground north, south, east, and west. Then I ran a string between two posts, north and south and then another string east and west. I made sure everything was square so that where they crossed would be a true center. Then I drew a circle around the center with a diameter of twelve feet. That became the center resting area of the maze. Next I placed dots for the seed pattern I had found online and calculated how to place them so that the paths of the maze would be sixteen inches wide. I used chalk first and then I used blue line paint, the kind you see on pavement for restricted parking spaces. It was a fun project and my oldest granddaughter Emma helped.

The history of mazes and labyrinths is ancient, stretching back to the time before Christ. The classical labyrinth with seven circuits is found on a coin from Knossos, Crete. The medieval period developed a more intricate form with eleven circuits, the most famous of which is found in the Chartres Cathedral near Paris, France. It was laid on the floor of this impressive cathedral which was built in the early thirteenth century and it has survived to this day. Maybe someday I will get to see it.

I like to welcome friends and family to our homestead. I like to cook, and I love to set a pretty table for a large group. Our house has a big table which seats twelve. Sometimes we can squeeze in fourteen or fifteen using some small but strong chairs which I inherited from my grandmother.

Two boards could be taken out to make the table smaller, but I like to keep them in all the time. A dining room table is not just for food; it is for crafts and sewing and games and homework and computers and anything else that requires a table. One time I collected a bunch of leaves in the fall and glued them into shadow boxes to hang on the wall. It turned out to be a beautiful collection which I enjoyed for many years, but unfortunately during the process the glue leaked through the newspapers I had placed on the table. Try as I might, I could not get rid of the marks left on the table. That was a disappointment, but I read somewhere that each scar on the furniture is a valued memory. And it has become one for me.

Over the years we have occasionally had large family reunions. Reunions always include food and lots of it, everyone bringing their favorite dish to share. The food is always delicious and the adults eat more than they should. The children run and play and get to know their cousins. I remember one time when we had a scavenger hunt, an obstacle course, and a piñata for the children. Jim's large family of three brothers and five sisters get together once a year for an extended weekend. For a number of years we met at Crystal Lake, a retreat near Mifflinsburg, but for the past number of years we meet at a school called Sharon Bible Institute in the summer when the school is empty. We sleep in the dorm rooms and prepare meals together in the large dining area.

"I wish we could skate on the pond," one of the children mused during some very cold weather.

"We need at least three days of this cold weather before the ice will be thick enough." Jim told them. When the ice was thick enough the children carried their skates down to the pond to skate. Unfortunately, it seemed like it was hard to get a good clear surface. Farm ponds usually need to be flooded to get good skating.

One year I tried to make a little skating rink in our back yard. Jim and I put some wood barriers up and covered the area with a large piece of plastic. We ran water into it, and we had a nice area to skate on but it was small.

"Mom, you must come out and try our sledding path!" my daughter urged me. I bundled up and watched the kids going down the lane, starting at the top of the hill. The dog would run beside them barking, but he didn't upset the sled. When I was a child, I loved to sled but somehow at this point I would rather watch. Snow makes a mess in the house, but we put a drying rack in front of our wood stove and all the wet clothes dry quickly.

Entertainment at the homestead was not the only entertainment our family had. We took a lot of vacations. When the children were married, the grandchildren started coming along, too. When we took a vacation together we would go to an interesting spot and rent a large house or cabin.

One year we went to South Dakota where we saw buffalo walking on the road near our cabin. Jim, always the risk taker, went bike riding and wasn't sure what to do when he encountered a large herd of buffalo. Fortunately, a park ranger showed up and Jim followed the ranger's vehicle through the herd to safety. We saw Mount Rushmore with its carving of the Presidents and some of the family managed to take a picture from a lookout point which made it look like one of them was part of the group of statue heads. Another memory from South Dakota was when we all wore cowboy hats and kerchiefs on a wagon ride.

Another summer we went to Durango, Colorado, and took a ride on the historic Silverton train. We visited the amazing ruins of Mesa Verde. A group, including our oldest grandson who was eight at the time hiked up Mt Sneffels. Some made it to the top, over 14,000 feet high. Mt Sneffels is one of Colorado's 55 fourteeners, that is, peaks which are over 14,000 feet high. Since then, our son Khris and his wife have hiked up 28 of the fourteeners.

Another year Seven Springs, Pennsylvania, beckoned. We went canoeing and tubing and one day the two oldest granddaughters and I made doughnuts at our lodge. One day we visited Falling Waters, Frank Lloyd Wright's famous house. It is built right over a stream complete with some falls which could be viewed from decks and balconies that jutted out over the water. The sound of the waterfall was lovely. I couldn't imagine living there, but the house was beautiful with lots of glass and planting beds full of flowers.

One year instead of going to a faraway spot we had our vacation at home right at our homestead. Of course, it was far away for some of the family who lived in Tennessee and Colorado. We went horseback riding at a nearby farm, and some of the family put up tents to sleep out in the woods a distance from the house.

Jim and I have taken several cruises with our married children and the grandchildren. A cruise to Alaska seemed to generate the most interest. We went on three cruises to Alaska, each time with a different family. The first one was with our daughter Rachel's family when we did the inside passage cruise and stopped at Ketchikan, Juneau, Skagway, and Prince Rupert. In Ketchikan some of the group took kayaks across the Tongass Narrow to nearby islands. There are no roads to these islands. The scene was peaceful and lovely. The group heard a looney bird calling—such a plaintive, haunting call. I bought a looney bird clock at a gift shop and for years I enjoyed its bird call as it announced the hours. For reasons I don't understand I loved its mournful sound. In Juneau, we took a bus out to the Mandenhall Glacier. From its origin on the Juneau Ice Field it stretched for twelve miles to where we were at the lake. Beside the glacier was a beautiful waterfall.

I remember when the cruise ship went through Tracy Arm Fjord, a thirty-mile inlet with towering snow-capped mountains on each side. It was very impressive! Our ship was too big to go the whole way to the glacier, but the turnaround of the huge cruise ship was spectacular to watch. Pictures cannot capture the beauty of this peaceful glide through towering mountains and floating icebergs. On deck twelve was a wall of windows. We enjoyed watching for whales which we spotted several times off in the distance.

We made another Alaskan cruise with our son Justin and his family with a similar route. This time our cruise ship did go to the glacier bay where we heard the sound of glaciers breaking off and falling into the bay. The sound was loud and distinctive, almost like the sound of a cannon shot or thunder! In Ketchikan we walked over the boardwalk built over the Ketchikan Creek. In Skagway we rented a van and drove five hours on the South Klondike Highway through the Yukon to Emerald Lake and back. Emerald Lake is a beautiful aqua colored lake; I have never seen anything like it. It is such a beautiful color. I also remember that some of us rented a car and drove inland to the Denali National Park where we took a bus tour up the winding road around the mountain and saw in the distance lots of wild animals including black bear, grizzly bear, mountain goats, moose, elk, wolf, and eagles.

A third Alaska cruise was with our two sons, Daniel and Khris, their wives, and Daniel's two little girls. Our daughter and her youngest daughter went along. This time when we walked the boardwalk built over the Ketchikan creek, we saw the salmon jumping over hurdles as they tried to go upstream for spawning. It is an amazing feat for these hardy fish. We also saw two sea lions swimming alongside the fish. Some of the group went on a rain forest hike and tour. In Skagway some went on a train ride into Canada over the White Pass. On the cruise ship we enjoyed the trivia games led by the ship's crew.

We went on a Caribbean cruise with our oldest son, Steve, his wife, and two boys. The cruise stopped in Florida, near Sea World Orlando, and in Nassau, Bahamas. In Nassau the group walked through the town and looked at all the wares sold by street vendors. The memories with our two grandsons include viewing fish via an under-the-water glass wall, touching a dolphin, and picking up a small lizard on the beach.

We did a cross Atlantic trip with our daughter Rachel and her family. We flew to England and Grandpa took three grandchildren on the London Eye (a famous Ferris wheel). We toured Stonehenge and each of us was given our own headset to listen to an audio tour as we walked around the huge stones. We stopped in France and our excellent tour guide told us stories about the Normandy landing during World War II. We went to the American cemetery where our daughter's husband had a great uncle buried. We stopped at Ireland, the Faroe Islands, and Iceland before the ship headed back to America. My daughter fell in love with the Faroe Islands. They are a group of islands under the sovereignty of Denmark. She loved the grand, treeless, silent mountains with sheep grazing on them, the quaint villages and the brilliant blue waters. We stopped to see the free-standing cliffs named "The Giant and the Hag." A small bus took us past small villages with a church and simple homes, some which had grass roofs. The bus driver told us that the people here live on milk and meat from their sheep and on the fish they catch. We saw a villager preparing fish to dry, hanging them on a rope.

In Iceland we found a cafeteria next to the visitor center where we all tried traditional Icelandic lamb stew. I loved it but some of the children were not fond of it. In Iceland we also explored a Viking village with stone walls and grass covered roofs.

We took a cruise along the New England coast to St Martins and Canada with our son Daniel, his wife, and two daughters. On the first stop we took a bus tour of Boston and Cambridge. We toured the Bay of Fundy and wished we could explore the caves along the high wall far out in the Bay. One village at which we stopped seemed to me to have been stuck in the past with quaint cottages and a small community that shared a meal together each Sunday morning after church.

Our grandchildren

Chapter 11

Selling Vegetables and Flying in a Private Airplane

"Contentment is not the fulfillment of what you want, but the realization of how much you already have." Motto found at a flea market which I have hanging in my kitchen.

For several years I joined a CSA group, Community Supported Agriculture, run by one of our relatives. I paid for my share at the beginning of the season. Then each week I would come and collect my share of whatever was growing that week. I liked this opportunity because it was like going to the store without having to think or plan. The first week I picked up a box of strawberries, a bag of mixed lettuce, a head of lettuce, a pound of greens (spinach, chard, kale), one half pound of radishes, 3 red beets, and 3 sticks of rhubarb. Each week there was a different combination of vegetables. Usually I found I could use whatever the vegetables were, and I was introduced to several new vegetables I had never eaten before, such as chard.

"I think I could run my own CSA," I told my husband.

"That sounds like an awful lot of work," he replied, "and where would you get the customers?"

I like to plan things, so I sat down and worked out a plan. It looked doable to me. I asked my grandson Joseph who lived nearby if he would like to help sell vegetables for money.

"Sure thing," he replied. Working for money was always a great idea to him.

I made up a flyer offering shares running 25 weeks (June 1 to Nov 17) for only $125. The advertisement read: "That's only $5.00 a week for some of the freshest and best vegetables you have ever eaten." We sold eight shares. I bought some baskets to put the produce in each week. And then the work began.

Each week I handed out a newsletter which included a recipe. I began my first newsletter with the following: "Today is the first produce picking day for our new venture. My husband, grandson and I are excited about this project. Every evening my husband and I walk through our garden, watching and enjoying each spurt of growth. The peas will be ready in a week or two, the cucumbers, corn, and summer squash are growing nicely and some of the tomato plants have little green tomatoes!"

That first basket included spinach, lettuce, green onions and mint tea leaves with instructions for preparing the tea and also a recipe for Spinach Salad. Our second basket had a few more vegetables—spinach, lettuce mix, kale, red beet greens, spring onions, tea, a parsley sprig, and a small container of mulberries. Each week I enjoyed filling the baskets and then I would take a picture of the basket. There is nothing more lovely than a basket full of fresh, colorful vegetables. But it was a lot of work!

The fourth week I wrote in the newsletter, "Today as my grandson and I headed up to the garden at 6:30 am there was a steady rain falling, and my grandson wondered if we shouldn't cancel it for today. No, I said that's not necessary, we'll just get wet and then change to dry clothes when we get in (I was glad I had picked the sugar peas last evening). But it had rained so much last night that when we got to the garden, we sank in the mud up to our ankles so it was difficult to move and our footwear kept getting stuck in the mud. Anyway, it was a good experience for Joseph."

Some weeks I had difficulty finding the five to six different varieties of vegetables I was aiming for. One week I used some homemade jam to help fill the basket. Usually I had no difficulty filling the baskets. We grew such a wide variety of vegetables and often a particular vegetable would be available for three or four weeks.

At the end of the season one of our shareholders wrote, "THANK YOU so much for the new, healthy, fun experience of participating in your CSA...You did a great job. Everything was tastefully clean and packaged."

The next year Jim and I were in the process of purchasing a new business—a personal care home—so we did not run the CSA. But several years later that urge to plan and grow vegetables hit me again after Christmas. So I made another stab at running a CSA.

Our daughter made up a beautiful brochure for us to give out to office workers, friends and neighbors. This time we only offered 22 weeks instead of 25 and we raised the price from $125 to $250. Instead of putting the produce in baskets we arranged it in trays and each shareholder would pick from the trays. This time we had five shareholders.

Two of my granddaughters, Emma and Abigail, live nearby, and helped me. They particularly enjoyed greeting the shareholders as they came to pick out their produce. We turned the covered porch under our deck into an attractive "market stand." I had a piece of lattice work which I hung on the cement wall and decorated it with plastic garden shoes filled with flowers. I bought long white trays with holes for drainage from a restaurant supply store. With six or seven trays holding vegetables on our long white plastic tables, it did look like a market stand.

"I brought a little gift for each of you girls," one shareholder told the girls one time as she handed each of them a lovely decorated homemade notebook to use as a journal. My granddaughters loved interacting with our customers. That is one of the joys of a home business.

We did not repeat the CSA the next year. I guess life just got too busy, and gardening is a lot of work. It certainly does have its pleasures though. Later, when I retired, I started the CSA again. I was feeling bored and looking for something to do. I love growing vegetables, so what better thing to do than to grow some for other people. To run a successful CSA requires a lot of careful planning and organizing which is something I also enjoy doing. I decided to offer vegetables for five months—June, July, August, September, and October. I made a list of the vegetables one could expect to have for each month. I was confident of the major vegetables which we have grown for many years: peas and beans, corn, potatoes, and squash. I was not as confident about the salad type vegetables such as lettuce, carrots, radishes, and broccoli. I decided that by growing those intensively in small raised beds and making many successive plantings I would be able to succeed with the salad type vegetables. I had a list of 25 vegetables I wanted to grow and planned to use mulches freely to avoid a lot of weeding. This small garden share business has been successful and very rewarding for me.

Jim heads a successful small law firm and he works long hours there. But he has often said, "You can take the boy off the farm, but you can't take the farmer out of the boy." He grew up on a large dairy farm, and he worked the farm for several years after high school. He likes tractors and tools and has spent many hours working the land here on our homestead. He plows the garden in the spring and then in the fall he rakes it. He likes to cut down trees and spends many hours every year cutting logs and splitting them, so we have wood to burn in our two wood stoves. At one time he split logs by hand with an axe but then he purchased a log splitter with hydraulic power that pushes the log toward a massive wedge which easily breaks the log in two. I often helped with the splitter. Jim would place the log to be split on the tray and I would push the lever to propel it forward toward the big wedge. He would carefully guide the log so the split would occur where he wanted.

Farm accidents are inevitable, and Jim has had his share. There is only one time when an accident resulted in serious damage. I had looked out the window and saw he was using the log splitter. I wondered if I should go help him, but he often said he didn't need my help when I offered. A little later I heard Jim coming in the front door.

"Lois, I just cut my finger off," he called to me in an anguished voice. I hurried from the kitchen. His face looked distressed as he was holding one gloved hand with the other gloved hand. He took the glove off and about half of his little finger was missing. For a trained nurse, I sure did not respond like one. I hit the panic button. I kept thinking that we needed to take the severed finger with us to the emergency room, but I couldn't remember if we were supposed to put it on ice or not. It did not bleed much at first, and he asked me to get something to wrap it in, and I couldn't think where to find the gauze or what kind to use.

I drove him to the emergency room with the severed finger wrapped in some gauze in a plastic bag and some gauze around the remaining finger. We were standing at the desk in the emergency room giving information and someone said, "You're bleeding." We looked down and there was a big puddle on the floor.

We had to wait a while for the doctor to come, at least a half hour. Finally, he came and examined the finger.

"Can you reattach the finger?" I asked him.

"No, the cut was too blunt and the edges are too jagged," he said. It took him a long time to prepare and pull the skin edges together. Then we went home, minus one half finger.

It healed well and never caused him many problems. He does say that one doesn't realize how important that little finger is for jobs like hammering or for gripping things. A lot of jokes have been made in the family regarding that missing part of the finger and the grandkids are always fascinated by it.

Jim upset a tractor several times. Once when it rolled Jim was unable to jump free, but a tree managed to stop the tractor before it crushed him. The last time he upset a tractor our grandson was working in the driveway and saw the tractor upset over a bank. Frightened, he went running down to check on him. He likes to tell us what Jim said when he asked if he was all right.

"I'm fine. Just get back to work!" his grandpa said somewhat gruffly. I think he was chagrined. He should have been.

"I can understand how a young person could upset a tractor, but why would an older man upset one," I asked. Jim just shrugged. Jim is somewhat of a perfectionist. When he is mowing near a bank, he wants to get as close as he can, so the mowing looks neat.

"I think Jim has had more accidents than anyone I have ever known," I sometimes tell people. He once upset a motorcycle and broke his ankle. He has metal in that ankle to this day. He cut his leg with a chain saw and it required stitches. He has had several car accidents; usually he rear ends somebody. He is always in such a hurry and patience is not one of his virtues. One time when he was cutting trees, he got hit in the head by a falling log which knocked him out just briefly. He was fixing the garage door opener one time and the spring hit him in his hand. That required surgery.

Jim always had a desire to learn to fly an airplane. When he was about forty years old, he took lessons and learned to fly. For about twenty-five years he and a partner owned a plane which he loved to fly. Even though I did not like to fly with him, I did do it for quite a while. Somehow while sitting in that passenger seat one just doesn't have the sense of being in control like the pilot has. I have noticed that a lot of pilots' wives feel the same way I do.

Jim is a risk taker. After a certain number of missed approaches and flying in inclement weather, I decided I didn't want to fly with him anymore. At first, I said I would only fly in good weather, but I started to realize that when you plan to fly, the weather is never good. In summer there are possible thunderstorms and, in the winter there are icing concerns.

"You have had too many accidents," I told him.

Searching for the Sacred

"I've never had a plane crash," he would tell me. I just decided that one plane crash would be one too many and I did not want to be along. I did miss flying with him though. We had some great experiences flying together, especially one trip we took out west to Colorado. We left on a sunny day in the middle of May from Lancaster airport in Jim's little Cherokee Warrior. At that time Jim had not yet received his IFR rating which meant that he was not instrument rated and could not fly in conditions which would require instruments; in other words, he could only fly when visibility was good. If bad weather came up, we would just have to wait for it to clear.

Our first stop was Allegheny County and we had dinner with our son Steve, who was living in Pittsburgh then. We spent the night at a Howard Johnson Hotel. The next morning we left Allegheny County and we stopped twice for fuel, once in Muncie, Indiana, and then in Kirksville, Missouri, before ending that day in Beatrice, Nebraska. Beatrice, which is pronounced with the accent on the "a", is a small city with a small country airport. We were fascinated by the area and we slept in a hotel there. The next day we completed our journey to Colorado, landing in Broomfield, and spending the night with Jim's brother John who lives in Colorado. Flying over the countryside was enchanting, and I liked landing in the small country airports. The little Cherokee Warrior would just slowly glide into the landing.

The next morning, we left Colorado and decided to stop again in Beatrice, Nebraska, for a fuel stop and to eat lunch. Small airports sometimes have available a "loaner car" and we were able to use their "loaner car" for a short tour of the city of Beatrice. Located in Beatrice is The Homestead National Monument. It commemorates the passage of the Homestead Act of 1862, which allowed any qualified person to claim up to 160 acres of federally owned land. The homesteaders were required to live on their land for five years and to cultivate and improve their property.

We spent that night in Bloomington, Illinois. The next day we were hoping to get home, weather permitting. We stopped for fuel in Richmond, Indiana, and then we stopped for fuel and lunch in Latrobe, near Pittsburgh. Latrobe is a small airport which the town built for the golfer Arnold Palmer. There are lots of small airports which private pilots like to use rather than the large airports. They each have a personality all their own. After lunch in Latrobe we headed back to Lancaster, arriving home in what Jim noted in his logbook as MVFR, which means "marginal visual flight rules."

Later, Jim wanted a faster plane and he and his partner bought a Mooney. Jim loved that Mooney but because it was a faster plane the landings needed to be faster also, so there was not as much room for any mistakes. It seemed more dangerous to me than the little Cherokee. However, I did fly with him in that plane sometimes. I remember a time we flew up to Lock Haven, a small-town west of Williamsport, for dinner. We took a walk along the river dike there. Because of the danger of flooding from the west bank of the Susquehanna River, the town built a large, beautiful dike there and the airport is right beside it. Lock Haven is also known as the home of Piper aircraft because the first Piper airplanes were built there.

Jim loves flying and has many memories of flights and places he has been. He has used his airplane occasionally for his law office clients. One time when we were vacationing with the family in western Pennsylvania, he needed to return to the law office for a few hours, and he took our son Justin and two granddaughters, Emma and Stella, with him. They were young at the time, and when I asked Emma what memories she had, she said she just remembered how loud it was. Small airplanes are not quiet like commercial flights. Jim and the passengers wore headphones so that they could all talk with each other. With the headphones on they could also hear Jim communicating with air traffic control.

Jim has also used his airplane to fly politicians. When Peg Luksik was campaigning for governor of Pennsylvania, she flew with Jim to some of her appearances and speeches. She did not seem to have any fear of flying in small airplanes. One time with Peg, Jim was trying to make a landing at night in the Pocono mountains and visibility was poor. At this time he had an instrument rating but the airport didn't have a precision approach. He made three VOR approaches but couldn't see far enough ahead through the haze to land. After the third time, a person at the small airport radioed him saying, "I'm going to turn off the runway lights. I do not want to see you splattered in the newspaper tomorrow!" So Jim had no choice but to find another airport. He went to Allentown where he could make a precision instrument approach.

Chapter 12

Building Tiny Houses

"Your word is a lamp to my feet, a light
to my path" Psalm 119:105.

Most of us don't know much about simplicity. We have more possessions than we know what to do with. One time I heard a motivational speaker say that every possession you have uses up valuable brain space. You think about it, you catalog it, you think about cleaning and repairing it, you organize it. To lighten your brain load, think about how to live with only half of the possessions you have and then DO IT.

There is a lot written about down-sizing and living with less. Perhaps one of the most obvious examples of this lifestyle is the trend toward smaller homes and even "tiny houses." My daughter was intrigued by some tiny houses she saw on the web. "Mom, you should build a tiny house and have Joseph (her son) help you. Dad is a good carpenter and you could teach Joseph some carpentry." My daughter knew that I was always up for a challenge. I started looking at the plans for tiny houses which I could find on the web and the stories about how ordinary people would build them. I decided to build a tiny house.

I bought a detailed plan and then proceeded to look for a twenty-foot trailer to build it on. Jim gave me advice. We found a trailer and I bought a plan for building a tiny house. I searched Home Depot and Lowe's for all the supplies on the huge list that came with the house plans. I spent a lot of time in those stores hunting for things and trying to figure out what I needed.

Building the first tiny house

Since Jim had worked for a carpenter when he was first out of college, he had basic carpentry skills. Besides that, he had grown up on a farm where the motto was "If you can, build it yourself," so he had built all kinds of sheds, chicken coops, and such things. He put the basic frame onto the trailer. We built the walls and set them in place. Then came the roof and we put a weatherproof paper on the frame, and it started to look like a house. I did hire several carpenters to help with the process, but I did a lot of the work myself and Joseph helped, although he would rather just climb all over the structure. It took almost two years to finish but finally we had a tiny house. I even furnished it. In the loft I put a fold up chair which could lay flat and be used as a bed for a child. I put a futon on the main floor which opened as a bed. Then I found a cute little table and two small chairs at Ikea. We put the house up in our woods but moved it sometime later when we decided to rent it to an enterprising girl who was starting a community of tiny houses in an old campground. Her business is doing very well; she rents her tiny homes out by the night and I get fifty percent of the income earned on my tiny house.

After we had completed the tiny house, I started thinking about how the design could be improved. I found a plan I liked much better than the first plan I had used, and I decided to build a second tiny house. This second house has two staircases which go up to lofts, which are located on each end of the house. The first house has only one loft with a ladder to reach it. I liked the staircases I designed; I think they fit very well into the plan. This second house seems more spacious to me although both the houses used a twenty-foot trailer. The bathroom is much smaller, but the kitchen area is larger. At this time, we are renting the second tiny house to a young girl who just finished school. She has it decorated very attractively.

It took a long time to build the tiny houses because both Jim and I had other jobs away from home. Jim worked long hours at his law firm. I was involved for 11 years as the major manager of a personal care home we had purchased from one of Jim's clients. When we bought the 70-bed assisted living type home we knew it had been run down; but we were hoping to upgrade it over time. However, we did not realize until we took possession that the state had just inspected it and had found 95 violations. At that time the state had become much more regulatory regarding personal care homes. So we were under the gun. I studied the situation carefully, came up with a plan, worked very hard, and within a year we had a stable well-functioning home that met state regulations. I became the administrator and found that with my background in nursing and business, the job seemed to fit my interests and skills. I had worked in long term care as a registered nurse and I had later become a CPA and started a small accounting business. But I did not like to work the kind of long hours that my husband worked because of my other interests such as building tiny houses.

I don't expect to build any more tiny houses, but I like to work with wood. Jim and I have put together many things with wood over the years such as a cold frame for the garden and several chicken coops. I found a book with plans for woodworking projects such as birdfeeders and children's toys. I am presently working on a bird feeder which is supposed to be squirrel proof. We will see—we have a lot of squirrels around here.

Over the years I have learned a lot about carpentry, and I can use basic tools such as drills and circular saws and even a "chop" saw. In my woodworking book, one of the projects I wanted to do called for a drill press. I bought one and used it for some simple holes I wanted to drill, but I needed to wait for my brother Lester, a skilled cabinet maker, to show me how to do more complex drilling. He made using it look so easy.

I made a simple "nail puzzle" toy which has ten nails which are to be balanced on top of a single nail. It is sort of a brain teaser. I also want to make a wind chime. I have always loved wind chimes and usually have one or two hanging on the deck.

Making things seems like a way of life on a homestead. With the garden and animals it seems like there is always some project calling, whether it be a new bean or grape trellis or a new pen in the barn for the animals. Building things and fixing things is a way of life. My husband has spent a lot of time fixing his equipment, especially his tractors and various implements he uses with them. Jim has a lot of tools and he says that his favorite store is a hardware store. After building the tiny houses, I am familiar with the layout of Lowe's Hardware Store, but I would not say that it is my favorite store. I think my favorite store is a garden store—I love to buy plants and flowers.

I have many hobbies and woodworking is one of them. Another is growing flowers. But reading has always continued to be an ever-present hobby for me. When I was reading Rolleston's book about the stars, she mentioned George Stanley Faber's book *The Origin of Pagan Idolatry*. That title intrigued me because I was familiar with *The Origin of all Religious Worship* by the skeptic French author Dupuis. Both these books were written in the 1800s. I bought Faber's book (which has been reprinted by Kessinger Publishing's Rare Reprints) and it took me quite a long time to plow through his 1500 pages of somewhat archaic English.

I have found that philosophers and historians seem to fall into two distinct camps. One camp believes the Bible is true and is a "lamp for my feet" and the other doesn't. Most modern philosophers do not accept the miracles of the Bible as being true. Some modern philosophers tend to be sarcastic of writers such as Faber who are in the "Bible is historically true" camp. Currently, it seems much of higher education discounts Christian beliefs, and sarcasm is a favorite way to do it.

In a nutshell the difference between Dupuis *The Origin of all Religious Worship* and Faber's *Origin of Pagan Idolatry* is that Dupuis believed that all religion was man-made and originated in the pagan religions which took their myths from the constellations of the zodiac and which worshipped the sun as the primary god. Faber believed that all religion comes from God and that the patriarch's worship had become perverted but still retained some of the original true worship.

The patriarchs (first men found in the Bible) and the pagans had similar worship places. Noah, Abraham, and Jacob built altars on mountains. The pagans did similarly, building their temples and altars on high places, either natural mountains or artificial high places. There are similarities between symbols and similarities in the style of worship services.

Perhaps the major resemblance between the worship of the patriarchs and the worship of the pagans was their practice of animal sacrifice. We find animal sacrifice in every country all over the world in ancient times. The central religious act in ancient Greece was animal sacrifices of oxen, goats, and sheep. Why did ancient men think this practice was so important that it was spread over the whole world? Is it possible that ancient men had a memory of God requiring this practice in the beginning?

Faber points out that the theology of Adam, Noah, and Abraham (Patriarchism) is the religion on which Paganism is based. He believes Paganism is perverted Patriarchism. As Christianity was built on Judaism, so Judaism and Paganism were both built upon Patriarchism.

Faber's ideas answered some of the questions I had had of why the skeptics felt that Christianity was copied from the pagan myths. Since the truth of God has flowed down through time, even though perverted, we can see remnants of the truth in all religions.

Several of my family members urged me to write this book, or I may not have had the motivation to do it. One of my sons, Daniel, was doing some research into our ancestry and DNA and he told me that when he looks at the names of our ancestors he thinks how nice it would be if we could have their story of what their life was like. Maybe someday, someone from my future generations may come across this book.

I wish you could stop in and visit me and my husband on our homestead. You could watch me planting lettuce or pulling up red beets. I could give you a pawpaw from our trees (if they are in season). Wherever you live, maybe this book will motivate you to enjoy some of the simple pleasures in life: grow a plant or vegetable, take a walk through a woods, or enjoy the antics of a chicken or a goat.

I believe that Christianity is true, and that Jesus Christ rose from the dead. Even though I find the evidence of this fact in the Shroud of Turin, we don't really need proof. Jesus told the doubting Thomas: "Because you have seen me, have you believed? Blessed are they who did not see and yet believed" (John 20:29).

Appendix 1

Sacred Strands
Introduction/Chapter 1
By Lois Clymer.
Published by Deep River Books

Introduction

Imagine a tapestry with the story of the world woven from the beginning of time. In this book we will discover the threads which will lead to the most important event of all history—the coming of the Sacred Promise, Jesus Christ, to redeem mankind.

These threads, the bits and pieces woven through history, tell of the promise of a Redeemer. We find this prediction of the Sacred Promise in the first chapters of Genesis in the Bible. We also find it in the constellations and in the ancient myths and stories and artifacts throughout all countries.

In the past three hundred years this message of a Redeemer has been disparaged by some. In the eighteenth century, several important philosophers and theologians began to question the validity of miracles. Genesis begins the story of a Redeemer and relates much early history. Nonetheless, a group of theologians called "higher critics" questioned if Genesis was a true historical account.

Modern archeology has done much to restore confidence in Genesis as true history. We will examine threads that support the fact of Genesis as real history. Some of these threads are bits of secular history, such as cuneiform tablets and artifacts; others are scientific theories such as the biological decay curve.

Some skeptics believe that Christianity is a religion simply copied from old pagan myths and mysteries. We see that thinking today in books such as *The Jesus Mysteries: Was the "Original Jesus" a Pagan God?* by Timothy Freke and Peter Gandy, published in 1999; and *The Da Vinci Code* by Dan Brown, published in 2003.

Can we prove that Christianity was not borrowed from pagan myths and mysteries? We can, by tracing the fascinating threads which show the story, the Sacred Promise, woven throughout history. The story of Jesus begins not in Bethlehem but at the beginning of man's time on earth. Some of these threads are the myths, the constellations of the zodiac, and other astronomical signs. Perhaps the most amazing threads of all are the threads of the Shroud of Turin—the burial garment of Jesus Christ.

As we explore the threads, we will look at ancient history: the early ages of Sumer and Akkad, Egypt, India, and Israel; and then the early history of Greece, Rome, Persia, and China. We will examine how these people lived, how they dressed, what they believed, and how the story of a Redeemer is woven into their myths and foreshadowed in some of their religious practices, including their animal sacrifices.

Ancient history is considered to cover the period of the oldest discovered writings, the cuneiform of the Sumerians, beginning around 3000 BC; and since some historians also include the classical world of the Greeks and Romans, we will place the end of ancient history around 500 AD, at the beginning of the Middle Ages.

In this book we will center on the event which shook the world—the crucifixion and resurrection of Jesus Christ. Beginning with the earliest history, we will look for predictions of a Redeemer and parallels to what we have read in Genesis. Starting with the account in Genesis, we will trace the thread of the promise of a Redeemer, the Sacred Promise, through the stories and myths of human civilization.

Chapter 1

The Beginning of the Sacred Promise

"Then Joseph could not control himself before all those who stood by him, and he cried,

'Have everyone go out from me.'

So there was no man with him when Joseph made himself known to his brothers. And he wept so loudly that the Egyptians heard it, and the household of Pharaoh heard of it. Then Joseph said to his brothers,

'I am Joseph! Is my father still alive?'

But his brothers could not answer him, for they were dismayed at his presence.

Then Joseph said to his brothers,

'Please come closer to me.'

And they came closer. And he said,

'I am your brother Joseph, whom you sold into Egypt. And now do not be grieved or angry with yourselves, because you sold me here; for God sent me before you to preserve life.'" (Genesis 45:1–5).

Genesis Tells of the Sacred Promise

Genesis, of the Old Testament, contains in its early chapters the oldest written history that we have. Genesis begins with the creation of the world and all that is in it and ends with the well-known Bible stories of Joseph and his captivity in Egypt.

In Genesis 3 we find the first mention of the Sacred Promise—the story of a Redeemer. The story begins with the serpent tempting Eve to eat of the tree which was forbidden. Eve tells the serpent that God has said, "You shall not eat from it or touch it, lest you die" (v. 3). The serpent replies "You surely shall not die!" (v. 4), and tells Eve that if she eats it, she will be like God. Eve eats of the fruit and gives it to her husband. When they heard the sound of the Lord God walking in the garden, they hid themselves. God called to the man, asking him where he was. Adam said, "I heard the sound of You in the garden, and I was afraid because I was naked; so I hid myself" (v. 10).

God replied, "Who told you that you were naked? Have you eaten from the tree of which I commanded you not to eat?" (v. 11). Adam then blamed Eve, and Eve blamed the serpent. God gave a punishment to the serpent, and to Adam and Eve, and sent them out from the garden of Eden. To the serpent he said, "And I will put enmity between you and the woman, and between your seed and her seed; he shall bruise you on the head, and you shall bruise him on the heel" (v. 15). Charles Ryrie, in his study Bible says the following regarding this verse: "Christ will deal a death blow to Satan's head at the cross, while Satan would bruise Christ's heel (cause Him to suffer)."[1] This verse is called the *protoevangelium*, meaning "first gospel." The seed of the woman refers to a virgin birth. In ancient times a birth was considered to come about because of the man's seed, so a birth from the seed of a woman would be a virgin birth.

Joseph Farah, in his book *The Gospel in Every Book of the Old Testament*, suggests that when Christ's heel was bruised, it may have been the natural result of crucifixion. In order to breathe, a victim of crucifixion needed to push his whole body up by the heel which was nailed to the cross, thereby creating a tremendous bruising of the heel.[2]

We find some of the following features in this story:

- Adam and Eve initially lived in a paradise (garden of Eden), where they communed with God and had a body which would not die.
- Disobedience to God caused them to lose their immortality. They now had a body which would die.
- God promised that through the "seed" of the woman, Satan's head (his power) would be bruised, but this "seed" would be bruised by Satan in the heel. This "seed" is Christ.

We can find the symbolism used here, that of the "seed" struggling with Satan and bruising his head, while being bruised in the heel, throughout history. We can also find other remnants of the story—that of Satan tempting Adam and Eve, and their lost immortality and lost paradise.

Because Adam and Eve sinned after the serpent's temptation, they and their posterity lost both life in paradise and immortality. However, a "seed" was promised who would defeat the head of the serpent (Satan), even though this "seed" would suffer in the process.

Archeological finds have discovered several ancient clay drawings which represent the first part of this story—that of the serpent tempting Adam and Eve to eat of the fruit of the tree. One of these clay drawings shows a man and woman sitting beside a tree, one on each side of the tree, and each is reaching an arm toward the tree while behind the woman is a snake. This ancient art is described in and also featured on the cover of Bill Cooper's book *The Authenticity of the Book of Genesis*. This "temptation seal" shown there is an impression from a cylindrical seal. It dates back to around 2200 BC and today resides in the British Museum, where it is known as ME 89326.[3]

There is also a hint of this story in one of the oldest known writings, *The Epic of Gilgamesh*. This epic is the story of Gilgamesh's adventures and his fear of death and search for immortality. In his search for immortality he goes to inquire of his ancestor Upa-Napishtim (Noah), who is now sitting among the gods. At the end of the poem, when he is told the secret of immortality, a plant and a snake are involved: Gilgamesh retrieves the plant, but it is snatched away by the snake before Gilgamesh eats it. Gilgamesh is unable to acquire immortality. The epic of Gilgamesh will be covered in more detail in the next chapter.

The Constellations Show the Story of a Redeemer

In the constellations we see the symbolism of the ancient promise of a Redeemer, portrayed as the conqueror of the serpent. Here we see, in picture form, the seed of the woman who would bruise the head of the serpent while being bruised in the heel (Genesis 3:15).

The first-century historian Josephus credits Seth and his children with the invention of astronomy.[4] Jewish, Persian, and Arabian writers also say that the family of Seth (Adam, Seth, and Enoch) invented astronomy.[5]

Seth was the son of Adam; and Enoch was the great, great, great grandson of Seth. Looking at the long lives of these three, we see that Adam, Seth, and Enoch would have spent three hundred years together. The long lives would have been an advantage for learning the cycles of the planets and stars. Enoch must have been a very godly man, as the Bible reports, "Enoch walked with God; and he was not, for God took him" (Genesis 5:24).

These very ancient men would have known that Adam lost immortality when he sinned and that a Redeemer had been promised—the conqueror of the serpent. We do not know what else God may have told the ancient men about this promise. This Redeemer, who would bruise the head of the serpent and thereby redeem man from the clutch of evil, would have been very important to them. It is certainly not surprising that they would have written the story in the sky, via the constellations. The constellations are formed of stars which do not, for the most part, resemble the symbol or figure for which they are named. Yet these same or similar constellations are found in all parts of the world, showing they had a common origin.

The ancient names of the stars, and the Roman and Greek myths which later became associated with the constellations, help to illustrate their message.

There are twelve major constellations which are on the ecliptic line, the circuit in which the sun appears to move through the sky in a year. Each major constellation is referred to as a "house," and each "house" also contains three minor constellations.

Virgo, Libra, and Scorpio, three major constellations, appear in sequence on the ecliptic line. They foretell the coming of the Redeemer. The constellation Virgo (see image), which has always been called the virgin, holds a branch in one hand and an ear of corn in the other. In her left hand, which holds the ear of corn, is Spica, one of the brightest stars in the heavens. Spica is a bluish, first-magnitude star, and its modern Latin name means "seed of corn." The branch held in the right hand is also found in other constellations such as Coma, Bootes, Hercules, Cepheus, Gemini, and Orion, and appears to have a meaning of "the one who comes." In the Old Testament, Jesus is referred to as the "branch" (Jeremiah 23:5).

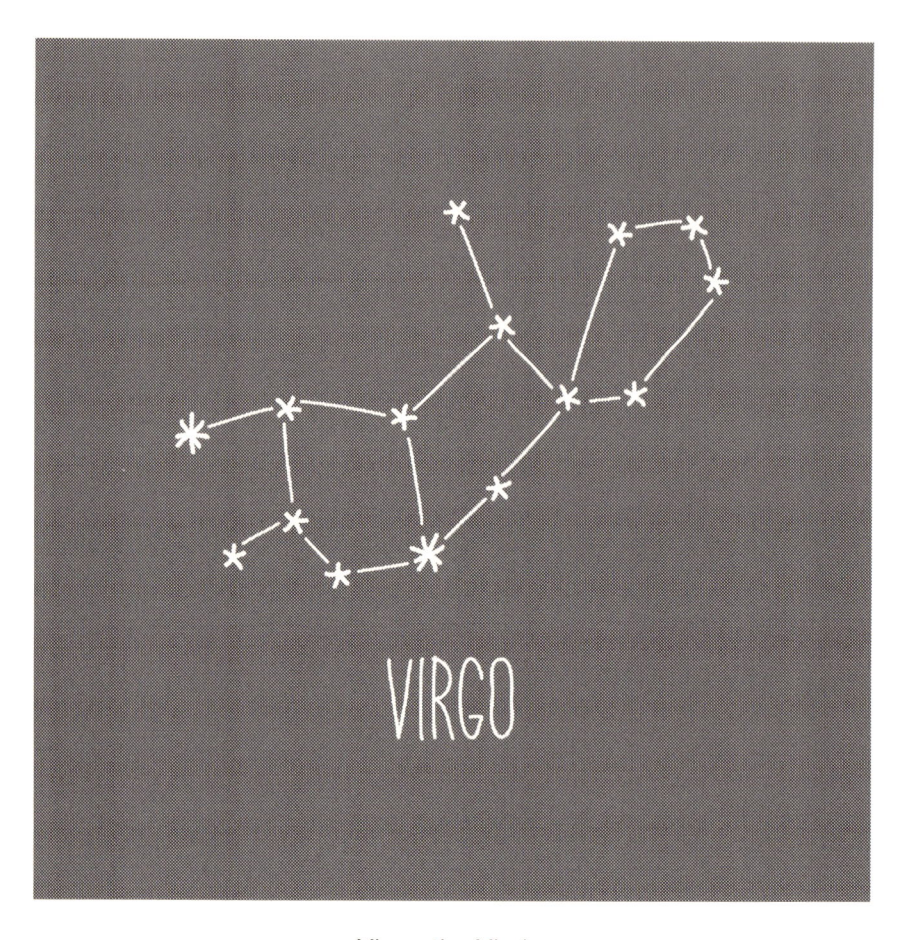

Virgo, the Virgin

One of the minor constellations in the house of Virgo is Coma, which in the old Denderah zodiac of ancient Egypt shows a woman holding a small child. Christians believe that this constellation prefigures Mary and the Christ child.

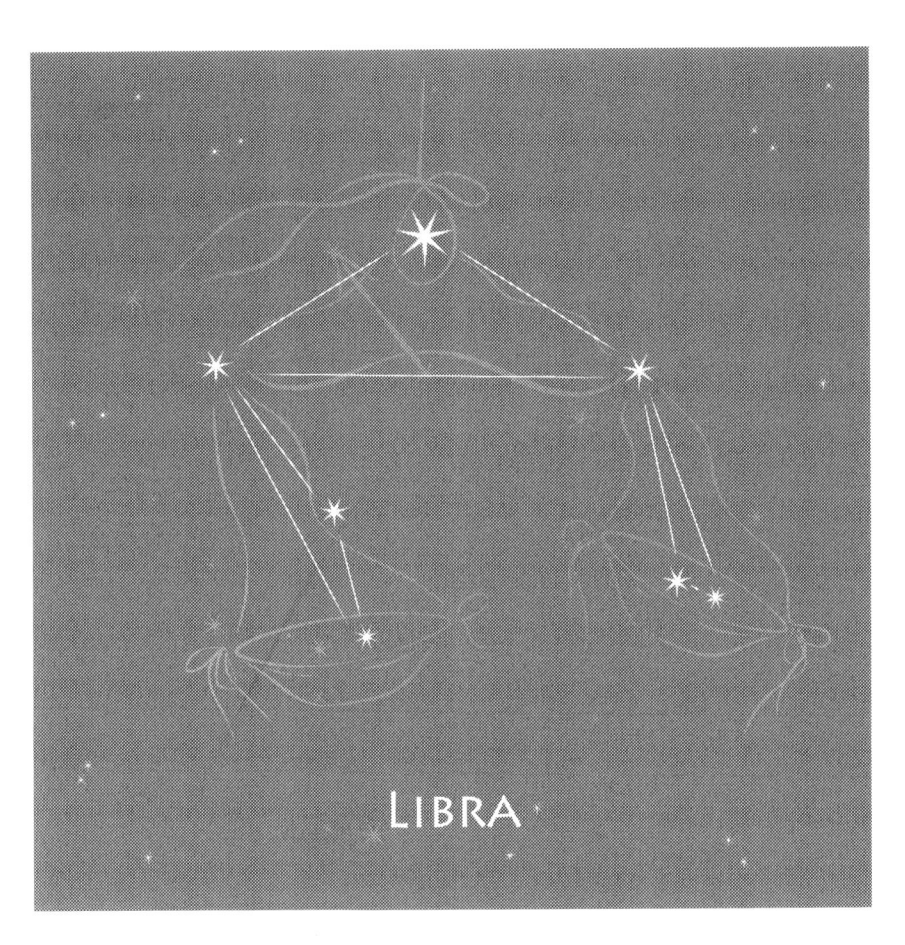

Libra, the Scales

The next sign along the ecliptic path is Libra, the scales (see image), suggesting a transaction to buy or redeem, showing the purpose of the Redeemer's coming. In Arabic, one of its star names means "purchase which covers." The earliest Persian planisphere pictured this sign as a man carrying a pair of scales in one hand and a lamb in the other.[6] A minor constellation in the house of Libra is the Victim, which shows an animal being killed by Centaurus, the centaur. Underneath the centaur is the Southern Cross, another minor constellation of the house of Libra, which in our age can only be seen in the southern hemisphere.

Ophiuchus, the Serpent Holder and Scorpio, the Scorpion

In the next sign, Scorpio, the scorpion, we see the conflict in which the seed of the woman receives the wound in his heel, while bruising the head of the enemy, as foretold in Genesis 3:15. Ophiuchus, the serpent-holder, is located right above Scorpio on the planisphere. Above Ophiuchus is the constellation Hercules. Both Ophiuchus and Hercules are part of the house of Scorpio. They both show the hero crushing the head of the enemy while being bruised in the heel. The names of the stars emphasize this meaning. The Arabic and Syriac names for Scorpio mean "wounding him that cometh." The serpent, held by Ophiuchus, means "accursed"; and an Arab star name in Hercules means "head of him who bruises."[7] Ophiuchus is struggling with a serpent. His one foot is near the head of the scorpion, while his other foot is near the stinger tail of the scorpion.

We see the same illustration with Hercules. Hercules has one foot on the head of Draco, the dragon, while in his kneeling position his other foot is lifted, as if hurt.

These three major constellations—Virgo, Libra, and Scorpio—along with their minor constellations show in picture form the protoevangelium, the "first gospel" found in Genesis. The virgin gives birth to the Christ child. The "conqueror of the serpent" (Christ) is bruised in the heel while bruising the head of the evil one. The constellations Orion and Perseus also show this theme of "conqueror of the serpent." The other major constellations appear to include elements of the story of a Redeemer, although some may be referring to future events, and thus are more difficult to interpret.

Job Predicts the Redeemer

The setting of the book of Job is in the patriarchal period. This patriarchal period includes the first men mentioned in the Bible up to the time of Abraham, who was born around 2000 BC. There is no hint of the nation of Israel, while several references in Job refer to the early events recorded in Genesis such as creation, the fall, the flood, and the dispersion. Job mentions several constellations, including The Great Bear, the Pleiades, and Orion (Job 9:9).

Job predicts the coming Redeemer: "And as for me, I know that my Redeemer lives, and at the last He will take his stand on the earth. Even after my skin is destroyed, yet from my flesh I shall see God; whom I myself shall behold, and whom my eyes shall see and not another. My hearts faints within me!" (Job 19:25–27). Job, living around the time of 2000 BC, knew of the coming of the Redeemer. In the midst of his suffering, he had the hope of the Redeemer.

We have examined the promise of a Redeemer given in the first book of the Bible, Genesis. This Redeemer would restore to man what he had lost when he sinned. The symbolic language used is that of a seed of the woman bruising the head of the serpent while being bruised in the heel.

Endnotes

Chapter 1

1. Charles Ryrie, *The Ryrie Study Bible, New American Standard Translation* (Chicago: Moody Press, 1978) 12.
2. Joseph Farah, *The Gospel in Every Book of the Old Testament* (Washington DC: World Net Daily Books, 2018), 6.
3. Dr. William R. Cooper, *The Authenticity of the Book of Genesis* (England: Creation Science Movement, 2011), 55.
4. Flavius Josephus, Book I of *The Antiquities of the Jews*, from The Complete Works, translated by William Whiston (Nashville: Thomas Nelson, 1998), 36.
5. Frances Rolleston, *Mazzaroth,* Kessinger Legacy Reprints (Whitefish, MT: Kessinger Publishing, 2010), 3.
6. William D. Banks, *The Heavens Declare* (Kirkwood, MO: Impact Books, Inc, 2013), 50.
7. Ibid., 64–73.

Printed in the United States
By Bookmasters